The Sista' Network

Property of
Project INSPIRE

The Sista' Network

*African-American Women Faculty
Successfully Negotiating the Road
to Tenure*

Tuesday L. Cooper
Eastern Connecticut State University

Anker Publishing Company, Inc.
Bolton, Massachusetts

The Sista' Network
African-American Women Faculty Successfully
Negotiating the Road to Tenure

Copyright © 2006 by Anker Publishing Company, Inc. All rights reserved. Printed in the United States of America. No part of this publication may be reproduced or distributed in any form or by any means, electronic or mechanical, including photocopying, recording, or by any information storage or retrieval system, without the prior written consent of the publisher.

ISBN 1-882982-92-4

Composition by Tanya Anoush Johnson, Senior Designer
Cover design by Dutton and Sherman Design

Anker Publishing Company, Inc.
563 Main Street
P.O. Box 249
Bolton, MA 01740-0249 USA

www.ankerpub.com

Library of Congress Cataloging-in-Publication Data
Cooper, Tuesday L.
 The sista' network : African-American women faculty negotiating the road to tenure / Tuesday L. Cooper.
  p. cm.
Includes bibliographical references and index.
  ISBN 1-882982-92-4 (alk. paper)
  1. College teachers—Tenure—United States.
  2. African American women college teachers—Professional relationships—United States.
  I. Title.
LB2335.7.C66 2006
378.1'2'08996073—dc22

2005021024

To my parents, Joseph and Victoria Hill.

Table of Contents

About the Author	IX
Preface	X
Acknowledgments	XIV

1 Introduction: The Challenges of African-American Women Faculty — 1

2 Tenure — 6
The Tenure Process — 7
Requirements for Tenure — 10

3 African-American Women Faculty in the Academy — 15
The Statistics — 17
Isolation, Mentoring, and Networking — 23
The Tenure Process — 27
African-American Feminist Thought — 29

4 The Research Results — 33
The Methodology and Structure — 33
A Roundtable Discussion — 39
   The Tenure Process — 43
   Collegiality — 54
   Service and Mentoring — 66
   Isolation — 77
   Networking — 89
   Highlights and Lessons Learned — 94

5 The Game of Tenure — 106
Learning the Rules of the Tenure Game — 107
Negotiating the Balance Among Teaching, Research, and Service — 109
Collegiality as the Fourth Category of the Tenure Process — 111
Finding a Mentor — 113
The Trilogy: Racism, Sexism, and the Politics of Singularity — 115
The Sista' Network — 118
Guiding Principles for African-American Women Faculty — 120

6 Conclusion: Six Years Later — 127

Appendix A: Research Design and Methods — 131

Appendix B: Sample Interview Questions — 137

Bibliography — 139

Index — 145

About the Author

Tuesday L. Cooper is associate dean of the School of Education/Professional Studies and Graduate Division at Eastern Connecticut State University. Before joining Eastern in August 2003, she served on the faculty at Springfield College. She holds a Doctorate of Education from the University of Massachusetts Amherst, a law degree from Western New England College School of Law, and a Bachelors of Science in political science from Rutgers, The State University of New Jersey. In 2001, she was awarded a Connecticut Community-Technical Colleges' Board of Trustees Minority Administrative Fellows position with Asnuntuck Community College. In addition, she has been awarded the American Association for Higher Education's Nellie Mae Scholarship and the University of Massachusetts at Amherst Teaching and Learning in the Diverse Classroom Fellowship.

Dr. Cooper is coauthor of *Diversity on Campus* with David Schuman and Carolyn M. Pillow (2004, Kendall/Hunt). Her research interests include tenure, faculty and department chair development, education law, civil rights law, and Critical Race Theory. She is a member of the Professional and Organizational Development Network in Higher Education.

Preface

I am a black woman who once had the desire to become a full-time faculty member. It was this desire that lead me to embark on this study—a qualitative inquiry into the lives and experiences of nine African-American women faculty during various stages of the tenure process. Audre Lorde (1984) suggests that if we do not define ourselves, we will be defined by others. Conducting this project provided me with an opportunity to take part in defining myself and what I had hoped to become. As well, the study allowed me to help define a "new" and more fully developed truth about black women in the academy (Collins, 1986; hooks, 1989).

I conducted this study to examine my past and define my future. In my former career, I was a lawyer. As a new attorney who happened to be a black woman, I was constantly reminded that I was in fact the reverse: a black woman who happened to be a new attorney. I was subjected to searches each and every time I entered a particular courthouse in the city where I practiced law. This would not have been a problem except that attorneys were normally exempt from being searched. I was often given the same response, "Well you don't look like a lawyer!" In addition, I was frequently in the company of other lawyers who referred to our black and Latino clients as "those people" who were in their stations in life because they simply could not do better. To them, however, I was an exception to the "those people" rule.

These could be racial incidents particular to the legal field, but I don't think so. It is my opinion that this behavior is indicative of behavior that plays out in the larger society. Since the academy is part of the larger society, I *expected* the same behaviors to be displayed within the boundaries of the hallowed halls of ivy. I was not wrong. I was curious about the degree and extent to which racism, classism, and sexism are played out in the academy, especially when race, gender, and class were wrapped up into a package: the black woman faculty member. I was also interested in the extent to which the combination of "isms" had created barriers to achieving the gold coin in a faculty member's career: tenure.

In addition to my personal biases, there are other limitations to this study. Since there are only a small number of black women faculty in American academe, I chose to send out a limited number of invitations to participate. I selected institutions that had more than one black female faculty member on the tenure track because I wanted to avoid making the institution, and therefore the participant, more identifiable than any other institution in the study. I also determined that from 20 letters I could anticipate roughly a 50% response rate. (I received a 70% response rate; however, some responses were received after my interviews were completed.) This would give me eight to ten women to interview, a manageable number to collect sufficient data to describe the phenomenon of black women faculty in the tenure process.

> Qualitative research attends to social, historical, and temporal context. Findings of these studies are tentatively applied, that is, they may be applicable in diverse situations based on the comparability of other contexts. (Mariano, 1995, p. 464)

A word about the sample group being representative of the overall population of black faculty is necessary at this point. It was never my intention to select a participant group that is representative of all black women faculty members. Qualitative research methodology does not require that a participant group, or sample, be representative. It merely requires that the group is large enough that data collection can continue until the data repeats itself (Mariano, 1995).

I did not include first-year faculty members in the study because frequently they have not had enough experience with the process. In general, much of their time is spent getting acclimated to the campus and the institutional climate.

I did not include faculty in community colleges because these institutions have a shorter tenure process. A faculty member can apply after only two to three years, compared to the six- to seven-year process in four-year institutions. The process is also less involved and does not place a great emphasis, if any, on research and publications.

I did not ask questions or focus on data related to balancing life outside of the academy—family, friends, and community—because research already exists that examines those areas. My intent in this work was not to duplicate previously conducted studies. As a result, traditional mechanisms for data collection and reporting were not used for this study. These alternative processes and the rationale behind their use are described in the book's appendixes.

The nine African-American women who consented to participate in this study are the rungs in the ladder upon which I once set out to climb to be a full-fledged faculty member. With all of its promises and perils, the gold coin of tenure is something most academic scholars desire. The Sista' Network—the relationships between and among professional African-American women faculty—is the way to make the process less difficult and less painful. Introduce yourself to black women on campus, who no longer have to go into the kitchen of the ivory tower to talk to one another. We now have a seat at the table, the conference table that is. It is up to us, and only us, to make sure we occupy our seats with confidence.

I have learned many things as a result of this study, and I am indebted to the women who participated. Because of their courage, I will not enter into the tenure process blind and unaware. I am not disillusioned with the tenure process. I merely recognize it for what it is: a game. It is an arbitrary process that leaves its players at the mercy of the whimsical moods of its former winners. The story would be different if the process was less arbitrary, more open, and did not rely on unwritten rules. But the nature of the game had its roots in an exclusionary foundation.

At times, this exclusion is based on traditional notions of who is perceived as qualified. As this book will show, *qualified* can be another amorphous, subjective, qualitative word that can be reshaped and further defined on a per candidate basis. Other times the exclusion is based on race and gender. Although most of the women I interviewed had earned tenure, they fought for it every step of the way. They had to fight their department colleagues, their schools, and the process. They had to fight to maintain their integrity, their honor, and their dignity. They had to fight (and some are still fighting) to be seen as professors and scholars. Most of all they had to fight themselves. They had to fight the urges to leave and abandon their calling. And each of these women has been called to the academy.

I left one profession because I had to fight arbitrary and unwritten rules, attacks on my qualifications to do the job, sexism, and racism. Regardless of the differing arenas, one thing remains constant—I am a black women. I can change professions. I can change location. I cannot change my race or my gender, nor do I wish to. Thus the burdens experienced by black women are mine to bear.

Tuesday L. Cooper
June 2005

Acknowledgments

I want to thank the women in my own Sista' Network: C. Zakiah Barksdale, B. Gina Joseph Collins, Barbara Crawford, Patricia Gratsy-Gaines, Denise Moody Lane, Daphne G. Moore, Lorraine Vance, and Cecilia Douthy Willis. In addition, there are brothers in the network to whom I am forever indebted: Artie Crawford II, Cheedy Jaja, David Schuman, C. James Trotman, and Raymond Vance.

I also thank the women outside of the network: Gail Centola, Patricia Kleine, Meg Kluge, Carolyn Pillow, and Mary Deane Sorcinelli.

To James Anker and Carolyn Dumore of Anker Publishing, thank you, thank you, thank you.

To Nia F. Moore, an up-and-coming sista'—you can do anything.

And I give thanks to the Creator, with whom all things are possible.

Introduction: The Challenges of African-American Women Faculty

"The colored woman of to-day occupies, one may say, a unique position in this country. . . . She is confronted by both a woman question and a race problem, and is as yet an unknown or unacknowledged factor in both" (Cooper, 1892/1995, p. 45). This statement highlights the intricacies of being an African-American woman in late 19th-century America, and it continues to reflect the status of African-American women in the early 21st century. African-American women still struggle with the "woman question" as it relates to traditional roles: women, feminism, and sisterhood. They also confront the "race problem." Issues such as tokenism, being representatives of the race, and whether to be called African American or black remain prevalent.

African-American women faculty are overworked and serve on a multitude of committees. They do more than their share of mentoring and mothering minority and majority (white) students. Yet there is still the expectation that they will conduct research and publish at the same rate as their white colleagues, both male and female, who don't have the same hypervisibility due to race and gender.

But even with this visibility, African-American women are still invisible in the academy. They are frequently mistaken for students, glossed over for promotion, and go unrecognized as intellectuals or scholars within their departments. They are kept out of the formal and informal networks, the primary information loops, especially when it comes to the information needed for the tenure process.

> I was confident that we could collectively find a solution to some of the problems of race, class, and sex in the academy; today I am doubtful that we will ever achieve that goal . . . the state of black women in the white university admits to grave disappointment, unfilled dreams, and deep frustrations on the part of most of the women I know. . . . After almost two decades of service in white colleges and universities, by dint of race, class, and sex, at best, black women and minority group others now experience themselves in the peculiar situation of outsiders within the white academy. (McKay, 1997, p. 17)

The dilemmas faced by African-American women in the professoriate are not new. Although African-American women faculty are few and far between in predominately white colleges and universities, their problems are not. Issues of divided loyalties, isolation, and other stresses confront these professors more frequently than their white counterparts (Benjamin, 1997; Fields, 1996; Graves, 1990).

Until recently, the literature concerning minority women faculty in predominately white institutions treated race and gender as separate and distinct issues (Graves, 1990). The literature that existed referred to minority faculty in terms of their racial or gender group, but rarely in terms of both. Most mainstream faculty literature treated all racial minority groups as one, without recognizing the different experiences among and between the groups.

The 1980s brought a small increase in the amount of literature written about minority and women faculty. However, in comparison to other groups (women and faculty in general), there remained a limited amount of literature on African-American faculty and even less research on African-American women faculty. A researcher had to piece together information in articles about women and minority faculty in order to get even a limited view of the issues faced by the African-American female professoriate. The literature provided an incomplete view of African-American women professors and was, more often than not, written by white women

(Johnsrud, 1993; Johnsrud & Des Jarlais, 1994; Olsen, Maple, & Stage, 1995).

In the 1990s there was an increase in the literature written by African-American women about issues they face in academe. This literature reflected the satisfaction and dissatisfaction with their research, scholarship, teaching, and their relationships with students, colleagues, and institutions. Fields (1996)[1] summarized the "morale boosters" and "morale busters" for African-American professors in predominately white institutions, stating that the academy provides African-American faculty with a sense of purpose, adequate financial compensation, opportunities for research and peer mentoring, and access to up-to-date campus facilities. Conversely and simultaneously, academe also leaves them with feelings of isolation and marginalization, threats to their tenure and financial security, disparate workloads, tension over affirmative action issues, and limited access to resources for research (Benjamin, 1997; Fields, 1996). This juxtaposition continues today.

Still, there is relatively little literature on black women faculty. Most of what was written prior to the early 1990s was done by white researchers and lumped black women into one of two categories: minority faculty or women faculty. However, what has been written by black women weaves in African-American feminist thought in some fashion. All of the books and articles found are consistent. Each finds that black women faculty are the most stressed, the least satisfied, almost the least represented, possibly the least supported, and the most overworked of all faculty in academe (Alexander, 1972/1995; Benjamin, 1997; Graves, 1990; Gregory, 1995, Malveaux, 1998; Peterson, 1990). What is not found is literature on satisfied, well-respected, and widely published black women faculty.

Benjamin (1997), Gregory (1995), and Moses (1989) write about the experiences of black women in the academy as students (undergraduate and graduate), administrators, and faculty. With the exception of these works and a few others written by black women (Cole, 1993; Fields, 1996;

Graves, 1990), the majority of literature about black women faculty does not use their own words or their own narratives to interpret their experiences. None of the works describe in depth the experiences of black women faculty during the tenure process. And what has been reported has mostly focused on the negative.

This book is different from the existing literature in that it is qualitative and proposes suggestions for success. It documents the continued existence of the unique struggle of African-American women in the academy. By merging three distinct areas of literature—tenure, the experiences of black women faculty in the academy, and African-American feminist thought—this book explores the phenomenon of black women faculty experiences in the academic tenure process as seen through the eyes of nine black women faculty at different stages of the tenure process and at varying institution types.

A few words about the language used in this book. I deliberately chose the word *sista'* instead of *sister*. Sister is a formal term to describe a female sibling, biological or by circumstance (marriage, adoption). Sista' reflects upon an informal but intentional relationship formed between women for the purposes of sharing time and friendship, also known as a sista friend. Johnnetta B. Cole, president of Bennett College, was often called the Sister President[2] when she was president of Spelman College because of the familial relationship she established with the campus community and others off campus (Cole, 1993).

I created the term *Sista' Network* to describe the relationships between and among professional African-American women that enable them to assist one another in learning the unwritten rules and protocols of various professions. The network is a combination of networking and familial relationships.

I liken the Sista' Network to the relationship between and among African-American people who escaped slavery on the Underground Railroad in the late 18th and 19th centuries (Franklin, 1974). Like the Underground Railroad, the Sista' Network can help African-American women to successfully negotiate the road to a freedom: academic freedom and financial security. The Sista' Network provides a path or roadmap for African-American women faculty to help each other negotiate the often lonely and treacherous road to tenure.

The terms *black* and *African American* are used interchangeably. This is done deliberately for two reasons. First, it reflects the continuing struggle in (and outside of) the African-American community over which term is most appropriate to define this group of people. Second, the literature and the women interviewed for this book used the words synonymously. In the context of this work, both black and African American describe people who live in the United States whose ancestry and culture can be traced to the continent of Africa.

Endnotes

1) The information contained in this and most articles concerning African-American faculty applies equally to women and men within this cultural group.

2) Although Dr. Cole uses the term sister, the relationship she describes in her book, *Conversations: Straight Talk with America's Sister President* (1993), is one of sista'-hood.

Tenure

In the academy, African-American women are forced to choose between several parts of their identity. Questions often arise about which part of their identity is primary; that is, being a woman, being African American, or being a minority. Rarely is it possible to choose to be just a professor. Nor can they choose to be African-American female faculty members because few exist in the literature and in academe, thus giving the appearance that African-American female faculty are anomalies (Locke, 1997).

> Many misconceptions surround the status of black women on campus, in large part because there is very little research specifically concerning black women in academe, how they are faring, and what issues are of concern to them. Research on minorities and women often ignores the unique position and experiences of black women. The result is that black women are virtually invisible. (Moses, 1997, p. 23)

Being an anomaly, whether welcomed or not, often becomes a hindrance when it conflicts with the activities that are required by most institutions to attain tenure. In order to explore the lives of African-American women, it is necessary to understand the literature in three areas: the tenure process in American higher education, the roles and experiences of African-American women faculty, and African-American feminist thought.

The Tenure Process

The concept of academic tenure has existed for several hundred years. It began in Europe as a mechanism to protect academic scholars from government and political intrusions. The concept was introduced in the United States in the early 1900s and became formalized by the American Association of University Professors in 1940 (Byse & Joughin, 1959; Metzger, O'Toole, & Glazer, 1979; O'Toole, Van Alstyne, & Chait, 1979). It has evolved into a system of policies designed to protect academic freedom, provide faculty job security, and create an elite cadre of professionals in the academy. Tenure is now perceived as the gold coin of faculty academic careers.

Although the tenure process varies from institution to institution, it follows the same basic structure. During a new faculty member's first month on campus, some form of orientation is held. Tenure and promotion information is generally distributed at this time. At best, orientations provide a general overview of tenure but give little detail as the initial stages of tenure and promotion vary from department to department and from school to school.

The second stage is an annual review or evaluation at the department level. The faculty member is asked to plan a research, teaching, and service agenda. Goals are reviewed and evaluated based on the success and achievements made toward reaching the set goals. Unknown to most, these annual reviews are used cumulatively for a mid-point review (often referred to as mini-tenure or third-year review). The mini-tenure process is more than merely a mid-point review. It can make or break a junior faculty member. It is here that the school or college dean may become involved in the process by reviewing the file and commenting in writing on each of the three areas: teaching, research, and service. The dean will note which areas need improvement prior to the tenure application process, which by now is less than three years away. During the fourth and fifth years there is generally a push to publish quickly and frequently in an effort to make up for lost time; publish for fear of perishing.

At year six, a tenure dossier must be prepared and submitted. There are three levels of review for this process: departmental, institutional (an advisory committee of faculty), and an upper administration level (the provost, president, or both). Each provides differing degrees of scrutiny. On the department level, faculty will be asked to submit several items documenting how their time was spent: a curriculum vita, copies of publications, student evaluations, a statement of research agenda, course syllabi, a list of peers and experts in the subfield who are familiar with the individual's work; all elements that show work activity and productivity over the six-year period (Goodwin, 1995; Leaming, 1998). This information will be reviewed by the department committee for content, quantity, and potential.

> The review will, in all probability, bring to bear a most highly focused examination of your accomplishments and promise. . . . The committee will almost certainly contain the senior professor in or closest to your own field. She or he will be asked to show how you rank with your peers, how your interests complement theirs, and how together as a team you cover the sub-discipline. . . . They will also testify to your qualities as a colleague and as an intellectual stimulus beyond the narrow coterie of specialization in your area. (Goodwin, 1995, p. 151)

The review is intense and painstakingly thorough. The overall question at issue is whether the faculty member has the potential to continue to contribute to the department. Goodwin (1995) explains further,

> The department will ask several questions. First, will you, over a lifetime, add to the reputation of the department? Is your research highly regarded by the field? Is it having a visible impact? Are you likely to remain productive? Is your success with students soundly based or is it rooted in a flash performance and the camaraderie of youth, which will not last? Are people a decade from now going to say "Oh

you're at State University, don't you have Professor X?" or will they say "Professor who?" . . . Whether you're a good colleague. Do you take on your share of the burdens of teaching, advising, committee work and other essential chores? Do you tolerate others? Do you interact effectively in personal and professional terms? (p. 152)

The institutional faculty committee carefully reviews the departmental assessment. This is purportedly a more objective process than assessment conducted on the department level. The administrative level serves the same function—an objective view cast upon the objective decision-making process of the institution-wide committee (Goodwin, 1995).

Whicker, Kronenfeld, and Strickland (1993) liken the tenure process to that of passing legislation in congress. They have developed a 10-point plan to guide faculty members though the tenure process. In sum, it requires tenure-track faculty to:

1) Create a personal research agenda and publish in peer reviewed formats.

2) View tenure as a political process: one in which faculty must manage cases and build coalition.

3) Find out the written and unwritten rules of tenure right away and take the initiative to find out specific information about tenure norms.

4) Save all papers and document any activity that is related to job performance.

5) View all promises made by department chairs and other administrators with suspicion.

6) Integrate research, teaching and service activities and seek out assignments for advancement whenever possible.

7) Try not to manage the department (or university) until after tenure is awarded, and do not neglect research and teaching in the name of service.

8) Contribute a fair share of work to department-based activities. Be, and be perceived as, a good citizen.

9) Acquire and maintain a professional image and share it with colleagues.

10) Develop a record that is tenurable beyond the current home institution.

Whicker, Kronenfeld, and Strickland (1993) acknowledge that this may not be an easy task for all faculty. "Gender and racial differences work against immediate entry into the informal power structures. Faculty with unusual life-styles, accents, habits of dress, and intellectual perspectives also may be separated from the mainstream and its informal information channels" (pp. 30–31).

Requirements for Tenure

Faculty must pursue teaching, research, and service in order to be considered for and to receive tenure. Teaching is traditionally defined as classroom instruction. Research is the investigation of new knowledge and truths. Service is defined as participating in a variety of activities to help better the institutional environment, student development, or community development (Benjamin, 1997; Burgess, 1997; Park, 1996).

Today, teaching encompasses more than classroom instruction. The definition of teaching has been expanded to include work both inside and outside of the classroom. There are different aspects of teaching, however, which are interrelated. *Instruction* takes place in classrooms, labs, clinics, studios, workshops, and retreats. *Advising, supervising, and mentoring* includes supervising student internships and fieldwork experiences, supervising graduate teaching assistants, career and academic advising, and advising students on research project theses and dissertations. *Curriculum and course development* encompasses redesigning and developing other learning activities. *Professional development* includes evaluating colleagues' teaching, conducting classroom and instructional-based research, and developing one's own teaching abilities (Braskamp & Ory, 1994).

Over the last 20 years, research has expanded beyond the investigation of new knowledge and truth to include publishing research results in journals deemed to be scholarly and presenting research findings at professional conferences. In the sciences in particular, all of these activities often are linked to one's ability to get grants to fund and sustain research (Benjamin, 1997; Burgess, 1997; Hawkins, 1979; Park, 1996).

The definition of research has also expanded. Writing textbooks, translations, and book reviews are now considered research activities, as are more creative endeavors. For example, faculty in the fine or creative arts may add writing novels, writing and directing plays, engaging in competitions, and displaying their work in exhibitions to their list of acceptable research activities. Research can also include editing books and journals and writing and managing grant activities (Braskamp & Ory, 1994).

The category of service, or citizenship as it has been called more recently, has also grown. Service can be in the form of service to the institution, such as serving as a department chair or other administrative post. Likewise, a faculty member can fulfill the service requirement by being an officer in a professional organization, (preferably one which sponsors a research-based journal within the discipline), or serving as a reviewer for such a journal. Acting as an advisor for a student organization or working with community groups counts as service. Community service can take the form of holding public office or participating in civic or political organizations (Benjamin, 1997; Braskamp & Ory, 1994; Burgess, 1997; Park, 1996).

However teaching, research, and service are defined, institutions weigh the three differently. Each institution defines these activities and dictates the order of importance. For example, research universities weigh research more heavily than teaching and teaching is weighed more heavily than service. Even within these categories, hierarchies exist

(Braskamp & Ory, 1994; Park, 1996). In the research category, there are subcategories as to which type of research is more heavily weighted. It is most prestigious and favorable to publish a theory-based article in a professional, referreed journal. It is less prestigious to edit and review for a professional journal or to publish in a magazine or newspaper (Park, 1996). Teaching lower-division or general education undergraduate courses is ranked at the bottom of the teaching scale but rated higher than university or public service. This is not the case in every institution, but it is the norm in research universities (Park, 1996).

In addition to those mentioned earlier, there are other rules for tenure, both formal and informal. According to Aisenberg and Harrington (1988), the "rules emanat[e] from a variety of sources—some decreed by tradition, others by the governing instruments of particular colleges and universities, still others by union contracts" (p. 387). The formal rules center around professionalism: teaching, research, and service. The informal rules focus on gender roles in academia, mentoring, balancing professional and personal activities, and negotiating institutional politics (Aisenberg & Harrington, 1988).

Institutional politics play an important role in the lives of academics, particularly academic women, because they often do not recognize that advancing in the academy is like playing a game. According to Aisenberg and Harrington (1998), in order to play the game one has to know the formal and informal rules. They suggest that there is one primary rule unbeknownst to most women: The tenure game is one of politics, not merit. The women in their study believed the opposite—that merit, and not politics, was the key.

> Women called themselves "naïve" and they mean that they did not—or still do not—know how to play the academic game, but they also mean that they rejected—or still reject—the idea that playing games to advance themselves is necessary. They believed—and still want to believe—that people advance themselves in the academic profession primarily through

merit. And by merit they mean true merit that includes quality of mind and moral commitment as well as performance in writing and teaching. Further they believe that true merit will somehow be evident and recognized by professional authorities without self-advertisement. They eschew academic politics—the technique of gaining the notice and support of important people—assuming that such game playing is, if anything, self-defeating because it is the opposite of merit and integrity. (pp. 393–394)

As a result, most women in Aisenberg and Harrington's study were not effective at playing the game. Employment term contracts were not renewed, and tenure was not awarded.

Another set of informal rules has to do with the "fourth" category for tenure: collegiality. These are unwritten rules, but in some instances they can be the most important aspect of academic life. Faculty members must not only be proficient in teaching, research, and service, but they must also get along with others in the department and in the larger university community (Whicker, Kronenfeld, & Strickland, 1993). It is helpful and seen as collegial if new or junior faculty volunteer to work with senior faculty on projects and department-based assignments. Failing to participate in these activities could prove to be detrimental to a faculty member's bid for tenure (Benjamin, 1997; Braskamp & Ory, 1994; Park, 1996).

These rules, written and unwritten, formal and informal, are in place because there has to be some mechanism for deciding who gets tenure. Tenure is an expensive and long-term commitment on the part of an academic institution. This is important because the economics of tenure are such that

> If we assume a thirty-five year duration of tenure until normal retirement age with annual compensation starting at $40,000 (and sure to increase with time and inflation), the employing institution incurs a commitment that will doubtless reach two million dollars. (Finkin, 1996, p. 128)

A multiyear financial commitment of $2 million or more per faculty member over the course of a career can be a strain on institutional budgets (Ruffins, 1997; Whicker, Kronenfeld, & Strickland, 1993). Such as commitment can prove astronomical considering that some larger state institutions have upward of 1,000 faculty members, approximately 65% of whom have tenure or are in tenure-track positions (Ruffins, 1997).

African-American Women Faculty in the Academy

The elusiveness of the tenure process has been problematic for most faculty. Historically, academic faculty were overwhelmingly white and male. Although the past three decades brought more women and ethnically diverse populations to the academy, the numbers were small. The problems, however, were large. As a result, the 1970s, 1980s, and 1990s brought an increase in the literature on these two groups of faculty. This literature suggests that pre-tenure women and minority faculty have very specific and unique problems in the academy and with the tenure process.

> We run the risk of grouping everyone together, as if everyone who is different is similar. . . . We do not intend to homogenize difference . . . however what all underrepresented groups face is an overriding organizational culture that is often formed on historical and societal patterns that are both white and male. (Tierney & Rhoads, 1993 pp. 63–64)

Various faculty groups, based on gender and race, view the professoriate differently as a result of varying experiences (Aguirre, Martinez, & Hernandez, 1993; Alexander-Snow & Johnson, 1999; Tierney & Rhodes, 1993). There is a common perception among colleagues that women and faculty of color have been hired to comply with institutional affirmative action policies (Aguirre, Martinez, & Hernandez, 1993; Alexander-Snow & Johnson, 1999; Fields, 1996; Moses, 1997). As a result, these two groups are viewed as less qualified than their white counterparts, or not qualified at all (Mitchell, 1983; Moses, 1997). Studies also show that colleagues are often uninterested in and nonsupportive of the type of research done by women and minority faculty (Fields, 1996; Johnsrud, 1993; Johnsrud & Des Jarlais, 1994; Locke, 1997; Moses, 1997).

Since women and minority faculty are often alone in their departments and institutions, they are frequently called upon to recruit new minority professors, serve on panel discussions, represent minority faculty views on campus, and advise and counsel female and minority students (Locke, 1997; McKay, 1997; Mitchell, 1983; Ruffins, 1997; Tierney & Rhodes, 1993). They are selected to teach classes about women and ethnic minorities because they are members of the respective groups (Mitchell, 1983; Tierney & Rhodes, 1993), unlike most white male faculty who are generally assigned classes based on interest (Mitchell, 1983; Park, 1996; Tierney & Rhodes, 1993).

Women faculty and faculty of color may *want* to teach, conduct research, and publish in the area of gender and minority issues, but they feel *compelled* by the department to do so. This is problematic because minority faculty feel forced to comply with this order (or responsibility), virtually without any choice. Although this dilemma appears contradictory, it is not. It is about expectations. These faculty want the option to teach and write about what they *choose* based on their interests, like many of their white male counterparts. They do not want to be perceived as experts or having an inherent interest in an area simply because of their gender, culture, or ethnicity (Mitchell, 1983; Park, 1996; Tierney & Rhodes, 1993).

Other studies of women and minority faculty show that individuals are hired and their contracts are renewed for five or six years. However, when it is time to be evaluated for tenure, these faculty are evaluated negatively and then must move to another situation (Blackwell, 1996; Johnsrud, 1993), a phenomenon often referred to as a "revolving door" (Park, 1996; Tierney & Rhodes, 1993). This is indicative of being in a faculty position with little stability or opportunity to advance (Carter & O'Brien, 1993; Gregory, 1995).

The literature confirms that the road to tenure is a difficult one for faculty members of all gender and ethnic groups. African-American women, who are members of both groups, have even greater difficulty in the tenure process. An examination of the limited but growing literature on African-American women faculty will demonstrate the reasons why.

The Statistics

> How was I to know that racism and sexism had formed a blueprint for my mistreatment long before I had ever arrived here? (Smith, 1983/1995, p. 262)

The tone of the literature and statistics specifically regarding African-American women faculty are grim at best (Benjamin, 1997; Carter & O'Brien, 1993; Fields, 1996). As shown in Table 3.1, African-American female faculty represented only 2.3% of the higher education faculty in this country in 1992. Even with a slight increase by 1999, the numbers still remained under 3%; a small growth, especially when compared to white faculty and other faculty of color.[1]

Table 3.2 demonstrates that between 1981 and 1991, more white women and faculty of color were hired to tenure-track positions than African-American women. The number of white women faculty in 1991 was more than 12 times the number of African-American women faculty on the tenure track. And although there was no growth in the number of white male professors, there were still 45 times more white male faculty than African-American women in tenure-track positions.[2]

The numbers are even more astounding when broken down into academic rank (Leap, 1995). Table 3.3 shows that in 1992, African-American women faculty in the United States were 14 times less likely to be a full tenured professor than their white female counterparts. White men were 74 times more likely to be a full professor than their African-

Table 3.1
Full-Time Faculty, 1981–1999

	1981	%	1991	%	1992	%	1999	%
Total Faculty	467,304		520,551		526,222		521,072	
Total White Faculty	424,071	90.7%	456,316	87.7%	456,761	86.8%	434,330	83%
White Male Faculty	313,600	67.1%	313,267	60.2%	390,945	58.9%	277,956	53%
White Female Faculty	110,471	23.6%	143,049	27.4%	146,816	27.9%	156,374	30%
Total Faculty of Color	23,565	5.0%	39,624	7.6%	43,676	8.3%	73,139	14%
Total Black Faculty	19,668	4.2%	24,617	4.7%	25,785	4.9%	25,935	5%
Black Male Faculty	10,532	2.3%	13,107	2.5%	13,682	2.6%	13,284	2.5%
Black Female Faculty	9,136	2.0%	11,504	2.2%	12,103	2.3%	12,651	2.4%

Source: Adapted from Carter and O'Brien (1993); the U.S. Department of Education, National Center for Education Statistics, "1993 National Study of Postsecondary Faculty"; and the U.S. Department of Education (see http://chronicle.com/prm/weekly/almanac/2003/nation/0102302.htm).

American female counterparts. African-American women faculty were two to three times more likely to be found among the ranks of associate and assistant professors than among the ranks of full tenured faculty.

Table 3.4 shows a slight decrease in the number of African-American women who have reached the level of full professor. But, the numbers at associate and assistant levels have increased slightly. As well, it can be seen that the numbers for African-American men have remained virtually

Table 3.2
Tenure-Track Faculty, 1981–1991

	1981	%	1991	%
Total Faculty	353,931		377,737	
Total White Faculty	232,256	91.0%	334,792	89.0%
White Female Faculty	75,100	20.0%	91,776	24.0%
Total Faculty of Color	30,675	8.6%	42,945	11.0%
Total Black Faculty	13,462	3.8%	16,170	4.0%
Black Male Faculty	7,516	2.0%	8,994	2.0%
Black Female Faculty	5,946	1.8%	7,176	1.9%

Source: Adapted from Carter and O'Brien (1993).

stagnant. However, when looking at the numbers for white women, the numbers at the level of full and associate professor have increased 4% and 5.4%, respectively.

In addition, Table 3.4 shows that at the level of full professor, faculty of color (Asian, Hispanic, and Native American) make up 11% of the faculty population. At the level of associate, faculty of color make up 14% of the faculty population. At the level of assistant professor, Asian, Hispanic, and Native American are 17% of the faculty.

Table 3.5 provides a view of the numbers among faculty of color. When faculty of color are compared to the larger population, African-American faculty are not the largest "minority" group in academia. Taking into account the numbers presented in both Tables 3.4 and 3.5, Asian-American faculty make up 5% of the total number of full professors as compared to 3% of African-American faculty at the same level. Both "minority" groups represent 5% of the number of associate professors and 6% of the number of assistant professors.

Table 3.3
Academic Rank, 1992

	Full Professor	%	Associate Professor	%	Assistant Professor	%
Total Faculty	161,252		123,471		123,285	
Total White Faculty	145,127	90.0%	108,408	87.8%	102,943	83.5%
White Male Faculty	122,068	75.7%	77,910	63.0%	58,560	47.5%
White Female Faculty	23,059	14.0%	30,497	24.6%	44,383	36.0%
Total Faculty of Color	16,125	9.9%	15,063	12.3%	20,342	16.5%
Total Black Faculty	5,160	3.0%	6,173	4.9%	7,151	5.8%
Black Male Faculty	3,386	2.0%	3,581	2.9%	3,452	2.8%
Black Female Faculty	1,774	1.1%	2,592	2.0%	3,699	3.0%

Source: Adapted from the U.S. Department of Education, National Center for Education Statistics, "1993 National Study of Postsecondary Faculty."

When compared to other faculty of color, African-American faculty are not the majority group within the "minority." Asian American faculty represent more than 50% of the population of faculty of color at the level of full professor. At the levels of associate and assistant, they represent more than 40%. African-American faculty are the second largest "minority" group, followed by Hispanics and Native Americans.

Table 3.4
Academic Rank, 1999

	Full Professor	%	Associate Professor	%	Assistant Professor	%
Total Faculty	161,309		128,826		137,791	
Total White Faculty	142,852	89.0%	109,037	85.0%	104,674	76.0%
White Male Faculty	113,304	70.0%	70,137	54.0%	56,463	41.0%
White Female Faculty	29,548	18.0%	38,900	30.0%	48,211	35.0%
Total Faculty of Color	16,950	11.0%	17,773	14.0%	22,999	17.0%
Total Black Faculty	4,784	3.0%	6,1462	5.0%	8,431	6.0%
Black Male Faculty	3,078	1.9%	3,601	2.9%	3,882	2.8%
Black Female Faculty	1,706	1.0%	2,861	2.2%	4,549	3.3%

Source: U.S. Department of Education (see http://chronicle.com/prm/weekly/almanac/2003/nation/0102302.htm).

There are several reasons why African-American women are not represented in great numbers within the population of tenured faculty. Some of the literature suggests that when there is an African-American woman faculty member in a department, she is usually the only woman of color, and sometimes the only person of color, in her department. As a result, African-American women faculty are frequently pressured by departments to serve as the minority spokesperson

Table 3.5
Academic Rank, Faculty of Color by Ethnicity, 1999

	Full Professor	% of Faculty of Color	Associate Professor	% of Faculty of Color	Assistant Professor	% of Faculty of Color
Total Faculty of Color	16,950		17,773		22,999	
Total Asian-American Faculty	8,786	52.0%	7,752	44.0%	9,718	42.0%
Total Hispanic-American Faculty	2,913	17.0%	3,161	18.0%	4,237	18.0%
Total Native American Faculty	467	2.8%	398	2.9%	613	2.7%
Total Black Faculty	4,784	28.0%	6,1462	37.0%	8,431	37.0%

Source: U.S. Department of Education (see http://chronicle.com/prm/weekly/almanac/2003/nation/0102302.htm).

on campus and advisor to minority students (Aguirre, 1995; Fields, 1996; Locke, 1997; McKay, 1997; Moses, 1997). They are also flooded with informal requests from African-American students to serve as mentors. All of this creates a heavy workload which takes time away from research and publishing; very important activities in the bid for tenure (Locke, 1997; McKay, 1997; Mitchell, 1983).

Once hired, African-American woman faculty are often viewed as products of affirmative action and therefore perceived as less qualified than their white counterparts for faculty positions.

> It has always struck me that in our country where second-class status is assigned to black folks and to women, the very last place African American women are thought to have the ability to excel is in the academy. After all, there is an incredibly tenacious stereotype that associates women with being emotional,

not rational; and there is the equally unfounded, but no less tenacious, myth that "because of our genes," all black folks are doomed to be intellectually inferior to all white folks. Thus, the last image that many Americans would have of an African American woman is that of an intellectual, an academic, a college president, a person of the academy. (Cole, 1997)

African-American women faculty often have to prove their worthiness and their credentials. This can create additional stresses for a new junior faculty member working toward tenure. The combination of racism, sexism, and the low number of qualified African-American female graduate students in the pipeline are additional reasons why these faculty are not faring well in white institutions (Gregory, 1995).[3]

These factors combined affect African-American women faculty when applying for tenure. Spending much of their time serving on committees and trying to prove their qualifications and worth to their colleagues leaves little time to prove themselves as researchers and scholars, a function that plays an important part in obtaining tenure (Aguirre, 1995; Fields, 1996; Locke, 1997; McKay, 1997; Mitchell, 1983; Moses, 1997).

There are two additional dilemmas facing African-American female faculty who work in predominately white institutions of higher education. The first is a feeling of isolation. The second is the issue of mentoring, its problems, and the role mentors play in individual departments, institutions, and careers in general. Isolation and fear can cause African-American women faculty to leave an institution. Mentoring can help them overcome isolation and help them stay.

Isolation, Mentoring, and Networking

There are three central issues concerning African-American female faculty and work experiences related to isolation. First, there is an effort within the department to choose where African-American women's allegiances and loyalties lie.

Specifically, the question often presented is, "Are African-American female professors members of a gender group or members of a minority group?" By having to choose sides, the African-American female faculty member is often isolated within an individual department and within the institution (Fields, 1996; Graves, 1990; Moses, 1997).

Second, there is a fear that their failure, any failure, will be viewed as if every African-American person has failed.

> This notion of either/or, the assumption that you must choose only one form of oppression against which you will struggle, is neither necessary nor helpful. Racism, sexism—sometimes we African American women cannot clearly tell where one ends and the other begins. But given the multiple ways in which racism and sexism are 'cut from the same cloth' we cannot afford to fight the oppression to which we are subjected only on one front. I like to make the analogy that if both of your arms were tied behind your back as you prepared to swim, would you choose to have only one released? (Cole, 1995, p. 550)

Third, African-American women are part of an ethnic group and a gender group. As a result, they often find themselves having to decide whether they are first female faculty and therefore interested in and supportive of women's issues, or African American first and therefore interested in and supportive of minority issues (Graves, 1990). It is rare for someone to directly ask an African-American female professor whose side she is on. It is more likely that the professor will be in a situation where she will have to choose sides. For example, will the African-American woman identify with feminist issues (as if all women are feminist) or represent the issues of people of color and other minorities (as if all African Americans are interested in issues that only affect African Americans)? This issue is important for two reasons. First, there are few people with whom African-American women faculty have a natural culture-based alliance (Fields, 1996). Second, in academe one must give support in order to be supported. Each choice brings its negatives and positives, and the group not chosen is often hostile and unsupportive for the remainder of the person's stay at the institution (Fields, 1996; Moses, 1997).

This situation often leaves African-American women feeling isolated from their colleagues and within their individual departments and institution (Fields, 1996; Graves, 1990; Mitchell, 1983; Moses, 1997; Turner & Myers, 2000). Despite myths to the contrary, this group is routinely left out of department decision-making, such as curriculum review and the hiring of new faculty, unless it is directly related to a "minority" issue (Aguirre, Martinez, & Hernandez, 1993; Fields, 1996; Locke, 1997; Moses, 1997). African-American faculty are included on committees that are formed to incorporate diversity and multiculturalism into a curriculum (Fields, 1996). They also are included on a search committee if the candidate desired is African American, Hispanic, Native American, or Asian. This concept is often referred to as *tokenism* (McKay, 1997; Moses, 1997; Olsen, Maple, & Stage, 1995).

African-American women frequently are not invited to lunch and other networking opportunities by white male colleagues who are often the senior faculty (read: the decision-makers) in the department. If the African-American female *chooses* to identify with her race instead of her gender, she may not be welcomed to networking functions by other female colleagues. This informal networking is the very crux of collegiality.

> Beyond the collegiality expressed by a few faculty members, I am invisible except for the important role that I play as a documentary, legitimizing a category for affirmative action purposes. . . . Faculty whose specialties are similar to my own (outside my department) rarely seek me out for exchanges or for symposia and such things. I work pretty much in isolation. (Moses, 1997, p. 31)

This experience is not uncommon, nor is it limited to collegiality or services opportunities. African-American women faculty are less likely to be approached for collaborative projects such as research, writing, and teaching opportunities (Fields, 1996; Moses, 1997).

For many African-American women faculty, the academy is an isolating environment in which they are overworked, constantly trying to prove themselves as academics, scholars, and more than mere tokens of affirmative action compliance. It makes sense to conclude, then, that they may receive less assistance from other faculty, or more specifically other African-American women faculty, to help them through the tenure process.

Mentoring and networking can help African-American women (and other faculty) to reduce some of the dilemmas and pressures of academe (Granger, 1993; Locke, 1997; Moses, 1997; Sorcinelli, 2000; Turner & Myers, 2000). Studies show that new and junior faculty fare better in the faculty experience and tenure process if they network, have a self-selected mentor, or participate in mentoring programs (Fields, 1996; Locke, 1997; Moses, 1997). "Mentoring is the key to breaking the glass ceiling among African American women. . . . Many African American women cite having a mentor as key to their career development" (Locke, 1997, p. 345). Mentoring programs and networking activities include discipline-based meetings, panel discussions and receptions, conferences, and other forums for faculty to express their concerns, and professional development workshops (Fields, 1996; Granger, 1993).

Participating in professional organizations provides an additional avenue for support and other opportunities for networking (Graves, 1990; Peterson, 1990). Several national associations have caucuses for different ethnic groups, genders, and sexual orientations (Graves, 1990). Since some African-American women feel more comfortable with a mentor who is also an African American, this presents an opportunity to network with women who look like them, who may share the same interests, and who more likely have dealt with similar dilemmas in academe (Fields, 1996; Graves, 1990; Peterson, 1990).

However, some literature suggests that it does not matter whether the mentor is white, African American, or a member of some other minority group (Fields, 1996; Granger, 1993; Johnsrud, 1993; Locke, 1997; Moses, 1997), nor does it matter whether the mentor is a man or a woman. What does matter is that African-American women have mentors within their institutions (and preferably within their departments) who are supportive, who view minority issues as important, and who will shed some light on and explain the tenure process clearly (Fields, 1996; Granger, 1993; Johnsrud, 1993; Locke, 1997; Moses, 1997).

Mentors help African-American women faculty feel less isolated and help them to prioritize actions and issues within their career development. Networking provides them connections with others in their disciplines who hold similar interests.

The Tenure Process

Most faculty hope to earn tenure, and African-American women faculty are no exception. Although institutions decide tenure priorities, the difficulty occurs when the candidate applying for tenure (in this case an African-American women) views and experiences the importance of research, teaching, and service in a different order than her department and institution.

African-American and white faculty view and experience the professoriate differently (Aguirre, Martinez, & Hernandez, 1993). In most institutions, whether research or teaching based, research and scholarship is the most important part of the tenure process. As a result, new and junior faculty are required to publish books and articles in well-respected journals in order to be considered favorably for tenure (Mitchell, 1983; Moses, 1997).

African-American faculty do not view research as unimportant (Locke, 1997; Moses, 1997); however, studies show that colleagues of African-American faculty are often uninterested in and nonsupportive of the type of research done by African-American faculty. They view it as pertaining only to minority issues (regardless of the topic) and thus not relevant to the population in general, unrelated to the discipline, and oftentimes unscholarly (Fields, 1996; Johnsrud, 1993; Johnsrud & Des Jarlais, 1994; Locke, 1997; Moses, 1997).

> There is an added obstacle of producing "acceptable" research and publishing in the "right" journals. Oftentimes white institutions and scholars feel that they have cornered the epistemological market. They tend to view research on race, gender, and ethnicity as not being "real" scholarship, particularly when it is presented from an Afrocentric perspective, and they have the same perception of journals that publish this research. Since research is an important component of tenure and promotion considerations, one need not guess the implications of such a perception of African American scholarly productivity. (Locke, 1997, p. 342)

As a result, the majority of African-American faculty have been "failing" in the research and publishing part of the tenure process. Some African-American women even feel compelled to write and publish two different sets of articles, one on gender and race issues and the other on issues more "relevant" to their departments and disciplines (Moses, 1997).

> I have gotten a lot of criticism about the fact that I am doing research [on social issues that affect black women in a cross-cultural context] that is not rigorous or relevant to the thrust of the department. . . . I have survived because I do two sets of research: one on black women's issues and one that is mainstreamed within my profession. It is the only way I will have legitimacy when tenure comes. (Moses, 1997, p. 32)

More African-American female professors favor the teaching and service part of the faculty experience leading to tenure[4] (Granger, 1993; Mitchell, 1983; Olsen, Maple, & Stage, 1995). In fact, they are likely to be on faculty at community colleges, teaching colleges, or less research-oriented universities (Graves, 1990; Gregory, 1995; McKay, 1997; Olsen, Maple, & Stage, 1995). It is unclear whether this is by choice or because African-American women faculty are viewed as unqualified, or less qualified, than white faculty.

While the literature does not suggest a reason for the preference toward teaching (other than to offer that African-American women were relegated to this area historically), it does offer a basis for the emphasis on service. African-American female faculty are often sought after by colleagues, department chairs, and higher-level administrators to recruit new minority professors, represent the minority faculty views in faculty meetings, and serve on committees, regardless of whether the faculty member is interested in that particular opportunity for service (Granger, 1993; Gregory, 1995; McKay, 1997; Mitchell, 1983; Olsen, Maple, & Stage, 1995). As well, they are frequently called upon by students to participate in panel discussions and to serve as mentors, counselors, and advisors (Locke, 1997; McKay, 1997; Mitchell, 1983). Serving as an advisor to minority students presents a unique problem. African-American faculty are role models to African-American students specifically because they are African American, regardless of whether the student is in the professor's class. This pressure from all sides often takes up a great deal of time which might otherwise be spent on research (Blackwell, 1996; Locke, 1997; McKay, 1997): "There is not a black woman in America who has not felt, at least once, like the 'mule of the world,' to use Zora Neale Hurston's still apt phrase" (Smith, 1983/1995, p. 262).

African-American Feminist Thought

> No one Black feminist platform exists from which one can measure the "correctness" of a particular thinker; nor should there be one. Rather, there is a long and rich tradition of Black feminist thought. Much of it has been oral and has been produced by ordinary Black women in their roles as mothers, teachers, musicians, and preachers. (Collins, 1986, p. S16)

African-American feminist thought[5], simply put, is the notion that ideas produced by African-American women can be used to explain the lives, ideas, and experiences of and for African-American women (Collins, 1986, 2000; hooks, 1989). There are several assumptions woven into this working definition of African-American feminist thought. First, race, class, and gender are inseparable. Second, only African-American women can produce African-American feminist thought. Third, although there is diversity among African-American women (age, sexual orientation, religion, class, ethnicity, and nationality), they share fundamental perceptions and experiences. Fourth, it is up to African-American women to help other African-American women understand and make meaning of their experiences using African-American feminist thought (Collins, 1986, 2000; hooks, 1989).

> Afro-American women's lives have been greatly affected by the intersection of systems of racial, sexual and class oppressions. However, they have developed a unique black female culture whose purpose is to foster authentic black female self-definition and self-valuation that counters and transcends the multiple structures of oppressions that they face (Joseph, 1988/1995, p. 464)

Collins (1986, 2000) suggests that African-American feminist thought has three recurring themes. The first is the importance of self-definition and self-valuation. Self-definition allows African-American women to challenge previous stereotypical, externally imposed definitions and images of African-American women. Self-valuation allows African-American women to replace externally imposed images of what African-American women should (or cannot) be with self-selected images. Self-definition and self-valuation permit African-American women to create their own standards for evaluating African-American womanhood and their own creation (Collins, 1986, 2000; hooks, 1989).

The second theme that reflects African-American feminist thought is the relationships between and among issues of race, gender, and class oppression. "While different sociohistorical periods may have increased the saliency of one or another type of oppression, the thesis of the linked nature of oppression has long pervaded African American feminist thought" (Collins, 1986, p. S19). Recognizing that there is a three-tiered dynamic that accompanies the lives of African-American women is an important part of understanding their struggles. Traditionally, African-American women were thought to be of one group, either ethnic (African American) or gender (a woman), and this was used as a point of contention to divide their identity and loyalty. Stating that race, class, and gender are inseparable lends credence to the unique roles that African-American women have had throughout history (Collins, 1986, 2000; hooks, 1989).

The third theme allows African-American women to redefine and explain their culture. This is closely related to self-definition and self-valuation. "Culture is composed of the symbols and values that create the ideological frame of reference through which people attempt to deal with the circumstances in which they find themselves" (Collins, 1986, p. S21). In other words, through the use of African-American feminist thought, the culture of African-American women can be redefined by the experiences and ideas of group members as opposed to being defined by outsiders' ideas of what the life and culture of African-American women should be (Collins, 1986, 2000; hooks, 1989).

> By and large the literature tells us that Afro-American women have a realistic, commonsense rational view of their relationship to the dominant society and do not operate on false illusions about their chances for survival or success (Joseph, 1988/1995, p. 464)

African-American feminist thought helps to put a cultural, racialized, and gendered perspective on the experiences of African-American women faculty in the academy. It is important that all black women faculty recognize that their race and/or ethnicity, the fact that they are women, their sexuality, and the class into which they were born (or are perceived to be in) plays a large role in their experiences as a faculty member, especially those trying to obtain tenure. Black women will have to balance these identities or make a choice as to which most, or best, identifies them.

A frequent phenomenon is the *institutional mammy* syndrome, whereby African-American women are seen as the nurturer of the children (students) and the housekeepers of the family (the department and the colleagues). In the academy, this translates to mentoring and advising African-American students (and other students of color) and taking on committee assignments that no one else in the department wants. It often involves having to work long hours and getting little reward for the time given. There is also an idea that African-American women faculty (the mammies) should be grateful to be in the academy instead of on the outside. Hence, the inequalities that exist—committee assignment distribution, course selection, late (or lack of) information about the tenure game and process—should be irrelevant because, after all, they could be housekeepers in the department, in the literal sense, instead of faculty members.

Endnotes

1) For the purposes of this book, the term *faculty of color* includes faculty of Asian American, Native American, and Latino American descent.

2) More recent figures about tenure-track faculty were unavailable.

3) Within the past several years there has been a relative increase in the amount of literature focusing on pipeline issues (Benjamin, 1997; Carter & O'Brien, 1993; Gregory, 1995; Mazon & Ross, 1990).

4) Unfortunately, the departments and institutions at research universities favor these two parts of the faculty experience the least. See Granger (1993), Gregory (1995), Mitchell (1983), and Olsen, Maple, and Stage (1995).

5) The term *African-American feminist thought* was coined by Dr. Patricia Hill Collins in her 1986 work "Learning from the Outsider Within: The Sociological Significance of Black Feminist Thought." Although, this specific term is not used in the works of other African-American writers whom I use as sources, such as bell hooks and Audre Lorde, their writings reflect the very heart of what Collins has labeled African-American feminist thought.

The Research Results

By presenting the research results included in this chapter in an alternative format, the voices of the participants are clear and distinct. The words of the women aren't clouded by the literature or the researcher's interpretation of the participants' thoughts and ideas. Instead, the readers can "hear" the participants' words in their own voices.

The Methodology and Structure

> But what fiction *can* do that no other sort of expression does is evoke the emotion felt, experience and portray the values, pathos, grandeur, and spirituality of the human condition. Pablo Picasso said that we all know that art is not truth. Art is a lie that makes us realize the truthfulness of his or her lies, (Banks & Banks, 1998, p. 17)

It is fair to say that Picasso knew a bit about art. He saw things differently, in the abstract, and pieced color together to make beautiful works of art. Arguably, there was an ounce of real life (truth) in his paintings. Perhaps figments of his imagination (non-truths) came together in some abstract form to tell a story that was clear to him, the artist, yet one which needed to be explained to his audience.

The same can be said about most writing, particularly fiction. Fiction is made up of a series of non-truthful pieces of information, fictitious characters and settings, woven together to create a story. This is done mainly for entertainment purposes. But fiction can also include historical data and other forms of factual information (truths) used to send a message to an audience (Bank & Banks, 1998; Kilbourn, 1999; Krizek, 1998). This genre of writing is commonly called the imperfect narrative.

For example, take John Grisham's (1996) novel *The Runaway Jury*. Admittedly a work of fiction, this book contains at least 100 pages of factual information (historical data, contemporary references, and statistical information) on the tobacco industry, courtroom procedure, and litigation. *The Runaway Jury* is fiction, a series of non-truthful events, settings, and characters woven together to tell a story, but it sends a truthful message about the dangers of smoking, the power of tobacco companies, and the shrewdness of litigation in American society.

This book can be considered semi-fictional in the sense that, although each of the participants was interviewed separately, the data collected are used to create a roundtable discussion in which the participants engage in a dialogue with an imaginary new faculty member. The roundtable discussion is inspired by the actual statements collected through the individual interviews with the participants. The story being told is only semi-fictional in that participants did not meet as a group to respond to the questions asked. The imaginary new faculty member is the researcher who posed questions to the group (as I did to the participants individually). In addition, where appropriate, I took the liberty to add opening statements to lead into the actual words of the participants. I added connectors to aid the reader and to enable the roundtable discussion to flow.

> The dialogue is a composite of various interactions written to represent the categories, themes, and cultural understanding uncovered in . . . ethnography. As such the narrative is fiction if fiction implies that the incidents did not unfold as specifically told. The writing of non-fiction signifies that the events and conversations as written are compressed from a

number of "real" interactions either witnessed or experienced. Be it technically fiction or not, I understand these people and the[ir] cultural world . . . and am writing to share that understanding. (Krizek, 1998, p. 94)

I interviewed the participants over the course of four months, but it took over a year to assess and make sense of the cultures within which they operated and to analyze the data collected. It became clear that their stories needed to be told. The question, however, was, how? How could I tell their stories in a realistic and innovative manner while still maintaining my intellectual and cultural integrity and that of the participants and this academic work? The imperfect narrative, as a form of writing, offered a solution to the dilemma. Banks (1998) suggests that the imperfect narrative allows a researcher to tell a truthful story in a fictional format, a crossing of genres. This permits the reader to be in the midst of the struggles in the lives of the participants/characters and not merely on the edges. When a researcher collects data (either through observations or interviews), it is done in context. The participants have lives and experiences that are difficult to relay as mere data on a page, in isolation and out of context. The imperfect narrative allows a researcher/writer to put the data in some sort of context or setting to allow the audience to better relate to and become involved with the lived experiences of the participants. It is an edgy, creative, and useful format.

> To accept "imperfect narrative" as a new means of reporting and presenting research will require the academic world to open up its disciplinary and methodological boundaries, and to question fundamentally accepted notions about reality, about truth, about lies, and how we express them. (Banks, 1998, p. 174)

Banks continues, offering a persuasive rationale for using the imperfect narrative (quoting Professor of Humanities Arturo Arias),

> The issue is not the genre, but again, the naming of the reality. . . . Sometimes, you see it in different ways and you find different means of expressing it. But to me it's all the same, and it doesn't really make a difference . . . because [all genres are] dealing with the same process which is naming that reality, recording it, and trying to raise the consciousness of its existence to the other people. (Banks, 1998, p. 175)

Odd as it may seem for a book based in research, the imperfect narrative is wholly appropriate for the intended purpose of this work. My intent is not only to tell the stories of the women interviewed, but to engage readers in the sharing of their lived experiences. In my opinion, merely reporting the data or just the facts is not the most effective manner in which to achieve my goal. The imperfect narrative allows me to create a story that is easy for the reader to follow.

This form of writing, while distinct, has not gone unexamined. More and more, scholars are beginning to recognize the importance of using fiction (and the imperfect narrative) as an alternative form within academic writing. Kilbourn (1998) offers two very convincing and rational reasons for its use.

> First, . . . the reason for [using] the alternative writing form was to give the reader a more tangible experience of a phenomenon. Good reason for the alternative form is to provoke such experience, if only vicariously, and it is tied to substantive meaning. Second, . . . there is clear indication of the [good] reason for the alternative writing, and it is explicit in the text. . . . These reasons demonstrate the self-conscious method. (p. 29)

Again, I submit that the use of the roundtable will give readers some insight as to the passion of the shared lived experience of the participants through the data collected. The potential staleness has been removed and replaced with a helpful, enticing dialogue.

Merely reporting the experiences in a matter-of-fact manner offers little; an isolated incident or two experienced separately by the participants. Once the dialogue is presented, the evidence is easier to see, vivid even. Each of the stories supports one another and weaves together a strong and intricately spun web of experiences that demonstrate the phenomenon. Reporting the data in the traditional format requires readers to work hard at spinning the web for themselves. The roundtable provides the completed web. Within this, readers move from being "passive recipient[s] of a descriptive monologue" (Krizek, 1998, p. 93) to active co-participants in the discovery of such phenomenon.

The use of imperfect narrative (or fiction) presents concerns for traditional scholars. Banks and Banks (1998) suggest,

> Fiction threatens the whole research enterprise. Research, no matter how qualitative and interpretive, rests on fundamental beliefs in reliability, validity, and objectivity, in reporting. When I say objectivity in reporting, I want to point specifically to the need for the narrative to be free of the research's imagination. . . . But [recently scholars] have bravely ventured into new narrative forms. Into storytelling that gives voice to Others, ... But even in th[is] experiment there's never any doubt that the researcher is telling about actual people doing actual things in the actual social world. (p. 17)

The data presented herein is reliable. I have triangulated the data (observation, personal experience, interviews, and the literature reviews). Its validity has been established through the literature review and the fact that I have spoken with (not interviewed) several other African-American women faculty who have had (and have heard of others having) the same experiences discussed here. Still, this is problematic for some scholars because there are very traditional ways of presenting data accumulated from research.

I submit that this semi-fictional format satisfies the requirements of an academic work. It addresses an issue that has not been previously addressed. It is clear and understandable, systematic in laying the foundation for the logical conclusions presented, explicit in detailing the implications of the findings, and thorough in covering the various aspects of the tenure process and the experiences of African-American women faculty. It is relevant beyond the participant group (Kilbourn, 1999). In addition, it demonstrates a self-conscious methodology that is necessary to aid the reader in following the author's ideas for the choice of format presented.

A self-conscious methodology is such that

> the author should explicitly demonstrate an awareness of his or her role as a writer [and] in some way make clear her or his sensitivity to the conceptual and methodological moves made in the presentation of the study as a readable document. The author should show an awareness of the bearing of those moves on the overall [intellectual] integrity of the work, should be able to give good reason for making them . . . [one approach offers] a solution that allows an author to demonstrate self-conscious method: direct explanation. (Kilbourn, 1999, p. 28)

Direct explanation provides an opportunity for the researcher to explain to his or her audience precisely the format in which the work is being constructed and presented. This is done so that there is no intentional misleading or confusion as to what the actual data (truth) is and what information is constructed (non-truth) for the purpose of telling a story. This is the methodology I chose to employ for *The Sista' Network*.

For example, although the dialogue is inspired by and representative of a compilation of the participants' words, I took literary license to introduce the speakers' words. One such introduction might include, "Let me say this . . ." or "The same thing happened to me . . ." The participants did not actually utter those words during our interview. However, the dialogue (as part of the roundtable) flows better and represents the way in which participants in a roundtable actually speak to one another. It must be stated that I recognize and respect the traditions of academic research. I have no intention of rebuking the traditional forms of reporting data and presenting scholarship, whether quantitative or qualitative. However, I recognize the limitations of both as that which can stifle creativity and innovation. My intent is to contribute a new voice to the scholarship in higher education, not to dismiss the establishment. Krizek (1998) recognizes this paradoxical situation inherent in academic scholarship.

> Scholarship, with its emphasis on acceptable forms of format, is conservative, yet its purpose is to generate the new, the innovative and the inventive. . . . [In] order to succeed [a graduate student must] do as they are trained, accepting the form and formats of their predecessor even though these conventions often restrict invention and strand in the way of innovation . . . (p. 91)

Recognizing myself as a change agent, I needed to utilize my voice to give voice to the participants in my research. It is nontraditional and unconventional, yes. It is a departure from the norm. No matter, it is also creative, scholarly, and unlike any other work produced on this topic. It fills a gap that currently exists: a merging of the literatures on tenure, black feminist thought, and the experiences of African-American women faculty.

In light of this, I must add that until the 1970s tenure was seen as a race, gender, and class neutral experience; an experience to be endured and not enjoyed. It was an experience that was difficult for all and absent of the "isms" within its process. This book ties those "isms" together, for a change.

A Roundtable Discussion

Thelma is a recent Ph.D. who is searching for a tenure-track faculty position. She is undecided as to whether she wants to be on the faculty of a research institution or a smaller teaching institution. She is also interested in finding out whether the fact that she is an African-American woman will have any impact or effect on her ability to succeed in the tenure game. While Thelma is clear that the tenure process is a game (she came to that conclusion while researching tenure for her comprehensive exam in graduate school), she is unclear about the extent of the unwritten, unspoken, but diligently followed rules.

Wilma is a senior faculty member and department chair at a large research university. She is renowned in her field and has published extensively on African-American women in the humanities. She received her undergraduate degree from an HBCU (Historically Black Colleges and Universities) and her graduate degrees from predominately white, elite universities. She has been tenured for 18 years.

Hope is a mid-career faculty member at a midsize state university. She is in the field of education and has published very little. She received both her undergraduate and graduate degrees at predominately white, elite research institutions. Hope is a mother and her family is very important to her. She has been tenured for approximately three years but did not receive promotion with her tenure award.

Jasmine is a junior faculty member at a midsize state university. She is an interdisciplinarian in the fields of education and social science. Although she hasn't published much, she has secured many grants for her department and has been recognized for outstanding service from a predominately white research institution. Jasmine is currently preparing her tenure portfolio.

Inez is a mid-career faculty member at a large research university. She is a nationally known scholar and has written well over a dozen articles, books, and essays. She received her undergraduate degree from an HBCU and her graduate degrees from elite research institutions. Her field is interdisciplinary, combining humanities and the "hard" sciences. Inez has been tenured for approximately two years.

Linda is a senior faculty member at a large research university. She researches and writes about African-American women and social issues. She is well published in her field and specialized in a subfield of the social sciences. She received her undergraduate and graduate degrees from predominately white universities. Linda has been tenured and promoted within the past 10 years.

Rachel is a junior faculty member at a large research university. Although she has not published a great deal, she has received university awards for her teaching. Rachel is in the social sciences and interested in race and economic issues. She received her undergraduate and graduate degrees at predominately white research universities. Rachel has passed the mini-tenure process and is looking forward to applying for tenure in a couple of years.

Eloise is a senior faculty member and department chair at a large research university. She is well published and is both nationally and internationally know in her specialized field combining the "hard" sciences and education. She received her undergraduate degree from an HBCU and her graduate degrees from predominately white research institutions. Eloise has been tenured for 19 years.

Wendy was a junior faculty member at a large research university where she was awarded tenure without promotion. She recently moved to a small liberal arts college and will be up for tenure at this institution in less than two years. In Wendy's specialized subfield in education, she is nationally known and well published. She earned her undergraduate and graduate degrees at large, predominately white research institutions.

Gayle is a mid-career faculty member and department chair at a midsize state university. She received her undergraduate degree from an HBCU and her graduate degrees from predominately white institutions. She publishes regularly and has secured many grants for her department. Her field is in education. She has been tenured for almost 10 years.

All of these women are African American. They live in the United States and were raised in different parts of the country. They are married, single, and coupled women. At least two of the women are lesbians; however, the degree of being "out" is questionable. There are some who were outwardly heterosexual and others for whom I could not determine their sexuality. If the participant did not mention her sexuality, I did not ask. All of the women are creative, intelligent, generous, and wise.

The task of describing these nine women is a difficult one for two reasons. First, they are all accomplished individuals who have contributed much to their respective fields and institutions. Reducing each to a paragraph does not do them justice; a book could be written on each. Second, most of these women have made such public contributions and are so well known in their fields (and beyond, nationally and internationally) that any further description would surely give away their identities. I have done my best to conceal their identities, hence each name is fictitious.

Their fields of study include literature, African-American studies, education, sociology, health, and history. Their publishing records range from a couple of works in press, to an article or two, to scores of articles and books. They attend conferences regularly, from the smallest regional conferences to the largest national and international conferences. They have held national fellowships, pre-docs, and post-docs around the country.

All of these personal and professional attributes and accomplishments are important to the women and to this study. These attributes and accomplishments are the very things that have been the basis of resistance from others, mainly their colleagues. Whether it was due to race, class, gender, or sexuality, these nine women have faced hardships in the academy that they have had to overcome. And overcome them they did.

I visited seven institutions. Four are large universities located in large urban cities, two are small universities located in suburban areas, and one is a small private college located in a small urban city. None of the institutions were Historically Black Colleges and Universities.

Thelma thought it best to go right to the source—participants in and survivors of the game of tenure. To do this, Thelma has enlisted the services of these nine women who are at various stages in the tenure process. She invited the women to a "Sista' Circle," a roundtable of sorts, to discuss workable and practical ways to negotiate and successfully attain tenure. She asked them a range of open-ended questions about the tenure process, collegiality, balancing multiple roles, mentoring, and the intersections among tenure, race, gender, and class. The discussion flows from their responses.

The Tenure Process

Thelma: I've asked each of you here today to help me sort out several dilemmas I am likely to encounter when I enter a new faculty position. I am particularly interested in the tenure process and whether I, as an African-American woman, will encounter roadblocks because of my race and gender. Any advice you have will be helpful. Why don't you introduce yourselves to one another?

Wilma: I've been tenured for eighteen years and I am a full professor at a research university.

Hope: I have been tenured for about three years, but I have not yet been promoted. I am at a small state university.

Jasmine: I am not yet tenured. I go up for tenure next year and I am also at a small state university.

Rachel: I am in my second year of a tenure-track position at a large research institution.

Linda: I have been tenured for several years at a large research university.

Inez: I have been tenured for about two years and I was recently promoted. I am at a research university.

Eloise: I am a full professor, tenured for about 25 years at a research university.

Wendy: I am not yet tenured at my current institution, but I was tenured at my former university. Tenured, but not promoted.

Gayle: I've been tenured for about 10 years and I just recently became a full professor.

Thelma: How would you define the tenure process?

Linda: I would say that it is a process of critical review of an applicant to determine whether the university wants to take that individual on for permanent employment. They determine whether they want to give that individual certain rights. It is a process of peer review and also of superior review; people who have already gone through this process deciding if they want you to be a colleague and to be part of the fabric of the university.

Wendy: It is a process where people on the outside are determining whether they want to take you on for life.

Thelma: Were you told at some point about this process and what was expected of you? In other words, when and by whom were you told exactly what you needed to do to get tenure?

Inez: It is interesting that you ask that question. I started teaching in September and I finished my dissertation in January. I had my first conversation about tenure that spring. I had conversations with my dean and my mentor and they were very general. My school is considered a "book" school. You have to have a book completed and maybe a published paper demonstrating some aspect of your new project before you will be promoted. We get promoted before we go up for tenure at my institution. There has always been some controversy as to whether it is a one-book or two-book school, and the dean did not clear up that controversy. Other people said it was quality, not quantity. I received a lot of conflicting information—it was very general and not very helpful.

Thelma: When was this?

Inez: It was during the third year. So that part I was very disappointed with because people did not give me a good sense of the timeframe. They did not give me a clear sense of what had to be accomplished and by when. At the beginning of my third year I had to have a book contract, but I was given no details. Do you have to have the contract in hand?

Do you have to have the revised manuscript done? I was not told whether I had to have a certain number of peer-reviewed articles. No specifics. I found that incredibly frustrating. But I got through that promotion.

Hope: At least you got something. At my school, during an orientation there was a brief presentation of the tenure process the summer before I started. Other than that, no one person sat down and talked to me about the tenure process. I spoke to a colleague on the telephone the summer before we started to submit our materials. She gave me some information. And the university sent out a mailing that essentially stated it was time to start thinking about the process. Mostly, I had to rely largely on my office mate, who was very conscientious and very into the process, to give me information. We were going through the process at the same time. Also, we have a school review (mini-tenure) which is not very involved. The dean usually writes a paragraph or two and it is usually based on information from your file.

Rachel: Fortunately, I had a colleague who helped me, too. We had a few informal conversations about how the process worked and what things would be good for me to do. He is a white male who is hated by a lot of the old guys. Since he and I share some of the same political views we've sort of become natural allies. But like I said, he is not well liked in the department. He and I are sort of on the margins together and we share marginal spaces. He is trying to help me prepare as much as I can for this process. It's kind of strategic. And certainly now that I am in mini-tenure, we've had a lot more conversations about it. My department chair has never talked to me about the process. I received a letter this fall from my chair saying that they needed certain materials from me by January 4th at the latest. That's the extent of my discussion with him about tenure.

Jasmine: We also had an orientation at my university and that is where I got a general overview of the process. However, there wasn't time for us to ask questions then. Every year we get evaluated based on a statement of expectations written when we first arrived on campus. This statement is compared to what has been accomplished over the course of the semester. During the evaluation process the department chair says, "Okay, this is what you need to work on or change for tenure. This is what you need to spend more time on." It wasn't until last year that our tenure and promotion committee put together a binder and listed the priorities under each area (teaching, research, and service). For example, what type of research is weighted more? Is it publishing? If so, publishing where? Is it grants or conferences? Up until that point, my fourth year, I had no idea. I had less than two years to get it all together. Since I had not previously published or hadn't published in the right journals, I was pretty much shot. Essentially, since receiving this information I have tried to get some articles published before my tenure packet is due.

Linda: At my school, you get one year contracts until your third year, then it's third-year review. This is much like the mini-tenure that Hope described. At that time the department decides—it's not an outside review—whether they want you to become a permanent member of the department. And so they review your work. Tenured faculty in the department review your work and talk to you about how you are doing. The more detail they can give you about your progress the better you end up. The group gives you an assessment of how you are doing, whether you are moving along. At that point people talk to you about your work in terms of teaching, publication, and service, but there's not really a sense of detail. This is when I had my first conversation about tenure, during my third-year review.

Wendy: Either my dean or my chair came to talk to me. However, I probably asked them long before they offered the information. It was during my first year. Neither the dean nor the chair had those discussions with anybody unless they asked, though. I was confused because I didn't know what the requirements were. I wanted to know how many publications I needed. No one would give me a straight answer. I talked to someone on another tenure and promotion committee and they said I needed two per year. I talked to someone else and they said one per year. Someone else said, "Well, just substantial or adequate publications." I was told, "You have to do good teaching, good research, good service." Later, the dean came to me about my teaching evaluations and told me what I needed to look at and improve upon for the tenure file. We put everything in files and he said, "I think you are doing too much service." I didn't mind my first year because I feel I got my questions answered. I knew what I had to improve upon.

Thelma: Wilma, did you have information early on about the tenure process?

Wilma: Each of my chairs, although they didn't walk me through the process, took the responsibility of preparing me for tenure. They would ask me where I was and they would suggest things that I could take advantage of in terms of opportunities in the department. I did not use all the suggestions, but they were helpful. My department was very supportive, very feminist in its orientation. My chair would tell me what was expected of me. I think I got two semesters off in the six years to pursue research. I should reiterate that I had more than one chair during my tenure process.

Eloise: Fortunately, I had assistance and lots of it. The dean and my chair came, looked at my annual faculty reports, and told me that there were a few things that I needed to look at, to improve. So they pointed things out along the way. However, I watched my sister go through tenure at another institution. She had to prove to this hierarchical committee that she was worthy of tenure. Her experience was horrible.

Gayle: The conversations were much more general. It was not a situation where someone came and said, "This is what needs to happen." My department chair and dean talked to me about tenure in a general fashion. However, several people talked to me about tenure. I want to be clear, though. They did not talk to me about how to get tenure. They mentioned that tenure was a game—that there was a game afoot and there were elements of that game that I probably should be aware of as I moved through the process. They explained there were things that must be done within the department, such as service. They stated I must form allies or at least neutralize those who may have decided for one reason or another that they didn't like me.

Thelma: Gayle, can you talk more about this game? What exactly do you mean by "There was a game afoot"?

Gayle: I can't define why it's called a game, but let me give you two examples of what I mean. My department chair decided that I wouldn't get any classes my first semester. His rationale was that in the department people chose the classes that they were going to teach and I wasn't there in the spring when the classes were chosen. He said that I would get to choose the next semester. What is important here is that I had to be visible in my department and on campus, and all of my work the first semester was somewhere else outside of the department, off campus—I work with student teachers. By the second semester when I needed to have my teaching observed, it was the first time I had ever taught the courses being observed. I didn't know how to interpret any of this, especially the "no class" part. At my institution, the process is that you get reappointed every year for five years. In the fifth year, you apply for one more one-year contract and tenure.

One thing that sticks out in my mind has to do with this white guy who was a lecturer when I got to the institution. He had not finished his doctorate, so he couldn't be an assistant professor. The school changed the rules and the next year he became an assistant professor. Follow me now. I was an assistant professor in the rank one year before him. I didn't get to see anybody's tenure folder beforehand. I did not get to maneuver the service opportunities. This young white male got any opportunity that came down through the department. When we did assessments, he became the assessment coordinator. This meant that not only did he get that opportunity, he got paid extra because that position was a paid position. He got to be chair of the faculty senate, which is a very political position. He got to be head of another high-profile service opportunity, another whole committee to run. Here again, I am talking about high-profile opportunities that he would get. Compare that to what I got: six students teachers who took me off campus. He would have the opportunity to get his name known.

I had a conversation with the chair and I said, "I have sat in this department and watched one person get an air-cushion ride and I have gotten zero opportunities. I don't even get a full load of courses to teach in the department. And here is a person who gets the courses, gets summer activities, chair of the faculty senate, and so on." The chair said nothing. So Thelma, when you ask did anyone talk to me about tenure, not only did they talk to this boy about tenure, they made a way for him. He finished his doctorate one day and practically got tenure the next. He got promoted to associate shortly thereafter and then he was full professor. He should not be a full professor if this business of rank is going to mean anything. I just got promoted to full professor, therefore he should just be coming up for full professor this year.

Thelma: He got it before you?

Gayle: Before me? He's been a full professor for about four years. Sure, he went to full professor I think before I went to associate. He had a very swift path.

Jasmine: They can be sneaky, or covert, shall we say. In my school, there is a junior black faculty member who is now looking for another job. We talk sometimes. During her first semester she taught a graduate course. There was this man in her class, posing as a student, who was asking her all sorts of questions about herself. She found out later that there was a part-time instructor in the department who had been sent there by the department chair to spy on her and to observe her teaching without her knowledge. Her office mate is also a black female. She went up for tenure and promotion and she got tenure but not promotion. The school told her she didn't get out enough and make herself known. It is interesting because when you get out and talk to people, in order to make yourself known, then they tell you you're out too much.

Wendy: At my institution, we got letters that were two to three pages, single-spaced from the dean, after the tenure and promotion committee met. Once we turned in our files, the committee would make comments on them. Then the dean would look at the file and give us a summary of what the committee said and his own extensive comments. He would even tell us the vote for our reappointment. I found this out when I got on the tenure and promotion committee. I also found out that the committee would usually select someone to vote against the reappointment if they wanted to send a quiet but strong message that something needed to be improved. If that isn't a game . . .

Inez: They will give you information when it benefits them. The second part of my tenure and promotion story is that my chair came to me and asked whether I wanted to consider going up for tenure early. And I was disturbed by that because there was no way I could have the second book done in time. But apparently my letters were really good. I know one reference said that if I was at his university they would have given me tenure already. My institution reconsidered and put me up early. I had to change my whole life and try to get as much done on the second book project as I could so they would have something to send out a soon as possible. This happened within a year of the decision for associate professor. It was very strenuous and very stressful and the most horrible experience. I couldn't sleep at night. And again there was very little support during the process regarding expectations about what had to be changed. The chair of my promotion and tenure committee, once I had him in place, was pretty good. He was good about the details, except he never gave me any lead time. We could be sitting here at 1:00 p.m. and he'd come in and say I have to talk to you right now. He'd say you have to change X, Y, and Z by 5:00 p.m. That is a lot of pressure.

Rachel: The game is more like a form of disparate treatment. I am almost convinced that I have colleagues, white colleagues, for whom the academy is not a foreign place because they have family in the academy. They understand its rules, they understand its workings, and they are coping differently than I am. For me this is all new. This is something that I am trying to learn and master at the same time, just like a game. It is very hard. I think there are rules of self-presentation and rules of prioritizing and all these things that I think determine, for white faculty members, the value of their colleagues. I think that making your own work a priority and being able to push off other people's needs are skills that are rewarded by academics. I have a harder time deciding that my work is much more important than some minority graduate student who is trying desperately to go through graduate school and to move on to somewhere else. To me, some of the "desperateness" of the students is important enough to put off my stuff. I don't think that white scholars see it that way at all.

Hope: Jasmine, I was thinking that your story sounded a lot like what happened to me. When I first started at my institution, I was told that tenure was pretty easy to get as long as there was a basic competency level within the three areas of teaching, research, and service, certainly with teaching having the greater emphasis. One would have to really mess up not to get it. I got tenure. I don't know anybody at my institution who has come up after me who hasn't gotten it. But there are other things that are more difficult; promotion, for example.

Thelma: What about promotion makes it more difficult to get than tenure?

Hope: The interview. I didn't do so well in the interview. There is an interview at the end of the process, after you have submitted all of your materials to a faculty committee. They make the recommendation whether to support you. I didn't do too well at that. It was a little tougher than I thought it would be, and I wasn't as assertive about myself and my accomplishments as they thought I should have been. And I definitely should have been. I left there feeling really lousy. They questioned everything I had done. And I guess I wasn't prepared for that. Some things I anticipated. I don't have much of a research background and I knew that. I anticipated that they would question that. But I didn't anticipate question in other areas.

I am not sure, but they weigh things differently. They are looking at a minimum level of competency for tenure. But we didn't have a conversation about that either in my department. In retrospect, it seems like we would have talked about that. I understand the standards have changed in recent years. I guess it's for the better. The school is more rigorous now that it was five years ago. People who got promoted five years ago probably wouldn't get promoted now. This is primarily because now there is greater emphasis on scholarship. I guess that is something that makes it more difficult than it was before. I think you have to be willing to commit many hours of time and money, forsaking all else. I am just not willing, or able, to do it.

Gayle: The first time I applied for a promotion, my chair came to me and said that she would not support me for promotion to full professor. In my mind I was thinking, "I probably should hurt her."

Thelma: Why are you all laughing?

Inez: Because we know the feeling.

Gayle: I had to apply two times before I was promoted to full professor. I had trouble when I applied for associate. When I applied for associate, the president wrote me a letter saying that my service quantifiably was not what others had who had applied for the position. At that point, I intended for him to have a hernia when he picked up the binder the next time I applied. It was going to be in a binder that was five inches thick so that when he picked it up he would think,

"Maybe I can quantify her service a little better." I am the type of person who believes that people talk about what they can get away with talking about. When I read the president's letter and it said that my service was the reason why he didn't want to recommend me for promotion, I didn't believe him because service is something that is easy for people to do at an institution. Service is about getting up, going, and doing. Scholarship is not about getting up, going, and doing. If he had said scholarship, maybe I would have understood. Scholarship is about digging it out, writing it up, and then getting someone to publish it. I worked flat out from year two through year thirteen. I wrote the president and explained my service to him. That was part of my strategy. I wrote them detailed letters asking them to sit down with me and tell me about the problem. So this process is you apply, you don't get support, you write a letter, you have a meeting, talk to the people, they stay where they are, and you go back in the next year.

The next year I applied for associate again. I think this time my chair came to my office and asked me if I planned on applying because she felt she could support me that year. I essentially turned in the same folder I had turned in the year before. I think I had had some article that was to be published and by that time may have been published. But essentially it was the same folder and I was involved in the same activities. She just had a change of heart.

Thelma: How do you learn the unwritten rules of the game?

Jasmine: You fall on your face and you get back up. Nobody tells you.

Hope: I didn't ask anybody. But I didn't even know I was suppose to get help. I guess you don't know that you are missing something until something has happened. You don't say how come I didn't know that or how come I didn't know this. I thought that if no one said anything and there was a lack of information that this wasn't a big deal. I assumed that if it was important, someone with power like the dean or the chair would tell me. So when it turned out that the lack of information was important, it was too late. Admittedly, it was mistake on my part. Maybe I should have taken more initiative, but I didn't know I had to ask. I accept responsibility for that. It was naïve. But how can you inquire about unwritten rules if you don't know they exist?

Inez: You are absolutely right. I think that it is the nature of a research university, any university, because it is upon you to find out immediately, when you walk in the door, what you have to do to get tenure. You have to go and seek out that information. You have to get those timelines and figure it out. That is the lesson I learned. No one is going to help you. In some ways I knew that. In other ways, it is hard to sustain that you have to be proactive all the time.

Collegiality

Thelma: Let's talk about collegiality.

Jasmine: Yes, let us talk about collegiality. Unfortunately, though it's not unusual, my experiences with collegiality also tie into race and gender. Sit back now folks, this will take a while. I have had five or so major, negative experiences with colleagues over the past four and a half years. Where should I start? I'll go in order. First, I was working on a search committee with a white male who had been at the institution for 30 years. One day, while he and I waited for a candidate, another faculty member on the committee, a white woman, walked in the room and asked him what he was looking at. He said my name and said he was looking at my breasts. And the woman laughed and told him that he need to get his eyes fixed or had to get a grip or something like that. I said to the man, "I cannot believe you could say something like that to me." He said nothing.

About two months later, and before I could decide what to do, there was another incident with a nontenured, white female faculty member. We were traveling together in a car to meet with a candidate, and we were talking with each other about the controversy over the "N" word because the NAACP was rallying to get it out of the dictionary. I brought it up with my colleagues because I told them that we had just talked about it in class, within a particular context. The white female said, "What is the problem with that word? I didn't know it was offensive. That was the word I learned to describe people of color. Is there another word I should have learned? What is the big deal?" I looked at her and said, "You have got to be kidding me." My white male colleague was less polite.

Later, when we got to the restaurant, we were talking with the candidate. I told the candidate that I had heard that he did a very good job on his lecture—candidates have to do a lecture during the interview. The candidate thanked me. My colleague, the same one who had made the comment earlier in the car and whose class the candidate lectured in, leaned over and in front of everybody said, "Well who could have told you that? It could only have been Ann and Teri (the only two African-American students in her class). So again, this is the mind frame of this teacher. No one else could have told me that because these are the only two students with whom I could relate and have come in contract with since the lecture. It could not have been any other students. It could not have been a colleague who told me about the candidate's performance. She singled out these two black students in front of everyone and called me out in front of the candidate and other colleagues.

About a week later we had a faculty meeting where all of the standing department committees had to give reports. I reported for my committee regarding recruitment and retention of minority students. First, some members of the faculty said that they weren't aware that there was a problem. Second, they questioned the validity of the survey used and the data collected. I felt humiliated.

I went back to my office and started typing a letter to my chair regarding both incidents that had previously occurred, detailing the events. I told my chair that the department was a hostile environment. I did not go to school for all these years to be treated like this. I didn't come here to deal with this kind of stuff. How could I be chair of a recruitment and retention committee and receive such treatment? How was I supposed to recruit people to come to the institution? I put it in her mailbox and the next day she called me and she brought me in to a meeting with the dean. They informed me that they had spoken to the male colleague with whom I had had the earlier experience. The next day he came in my office and apologized to me. He stated that what he did was inappropriate. He asked if I wanted him to stay out of my way. I told him no because I don't want to work like that, in that environment, because he screwed up. He went on with his business and I went on with mine.

By the end of the next month, the candidates had left campus so my chair talked to the white female. They didn't talk to her before because they didn't want her to blow up while the candidates were on campus. She said she wasn't apologizing to anybody for anything because she didn't think that she did anything wrong. She stopped speaking to me. At the end of the semester, the dean told me that they had spoken with her and she wasn't responding. During the first week of school the following fall, the dean said he wanted to meet with me. This issue was unresolved. He said, "I have spoken to her twice. The chair has spoken to her and the union representative spoke to her. And she still says she didn't do anything wrong. She spoke to a lawyer outside of the university regarding her rights to tenure. Now the ball is back in your court and you need to decide what you want to do. Do you want to go forward with a complaint to make her sit down for mediation?" I said, "No. The ball is not in my court; it is in yours. I did my part. I told you all what happened. You all let a nontenured faculty member tell you to kiss her butt in so many words." Now this says a lot to me about authority.

If all those people had come and talked to me, I would have been scared to death. I would have run and polished up. Why did I need to file a complaint? Why did I need to ask her for a meeting to discuss her behavior? I told the dean no, that it was no longer my issue. I had released it. This was their issue because she was defying them, not me. I was basically told that this had pissed them off and that there were other things they could do to get her back. I am not sure what those other things are. I know that a person in administration found out about it and she decided to call a meeting with the provost, our dean, and others. I heard from someone in personnel that time had elapsed so they couldn't do anything about it now. There were not a lot of options left.

I told the dean and the department chair that I didn't need this stress. They failed me. They expected me to recruit faculty for them and they failed me. This was a month and a half ago. Last week I get a call from the dean again, he wants to meet with me. What now? Apparently, the dean can still file a complaint even if I don't want to. The meeting was canceled, though, because the white faculty member has a lawyer and all meetings have been put on hold. How ugly is that? This is the environment I go into everyday. This is what I deal with. Now make that three people; something else happened.

I worked with a few colleagues on a grant for inner-city children and we were on an outing with the children. One of the faculty members volunteered his home for the outing site. The colleague, a white male, showed the kids from the inner city what I considered to be inappropriate videos that he wouldn't let his own kids watch. His kids said they were asked out of the room when the videos were shown. When we got back to campus, I sent him a letter and said, "What you did was inappropriate." I asked him why he would bring those kids out to his home to show them something that he wouldn't show his own kids. I received backlash from that. He stopped speaking to me. The kicker is that he had to evaluate my class, my teaching, and he ripped me apart. I sent him another note telling him that his evaluation wasn't about my teaching because I gave the same lecture the year before and he gave it a great evaluation. I wrote it up and put it in my file. The group never came to work with me again because I spoke up. And then it's looked upon negatively for tenure when you do research outside your department, because you should do research with those in your department first. But I have no desire to work with any of them. So the following year I wrote a grant and did the same program with people in administration. It worked well.

Gayle: I always document what has happened to me. I always ask questions. I always call for meetings. On one occasion, I thought my teaching was being observed without my knowledge. I wrote another letter requesting a meeting. One person told me that she wasn't going to meet with me. So I knew she was a coward. The person who voted against me during the promotion process told me that she wasn't going to meet with me without a lawyer because she knew my husband was a lawyer. So I put it out there. I said to her that I wanted to know how it was that I was being observed and I didn't know that I was being observed. I knew that I was observed because the faculty member on the promotion committee who had raised the charges about whether I was an effective teacher had never, to my knowledge, seen me teach. I wanted to know if I was being observed all the time, some of the time, or what.

One of the things that had to happen in this experience is that I took charge of the situation. There is a sense that there had to be a confrontation and a street fight all of the time. I had to be willing to say, "What is it that you want me to do?" I took my pinky out of the air, stopped trying to be collegial.

I felt like I had to take that kind of position. Not that everyone has to fight, but I don't think that I should have to be grateful to anybody and tolerate the type of treatment I received. I had to work hard. My credentials are what they are, and therefore I know what I am doing. Therefore being black and having a job, my university is not something I should be anymore delighted by than anybody else who is there. In other words, respect me!

I know there is a political aspect. I would work with someone who was supposed to be a nonsupporter. I would get on a committee with that person so it would be a face-to-face situation. I wouldn't back away. As a result of this, and the fact that someone who was an advocate and a champion for me was on the committee, the tenure process went swimmingly. Besides working like a dog and covering all of the bases, the other part of the politics is that you really have to have some type of advocate somewhere along line. I am not saying that it would never have happened if I didn't have an advocate, but that process is just iffy. If you can turn in the same promotion folder for two years and be rejected one year and promoted the next, it's not about the folder. It is about another dynamic, whether somebody will support you or won't support you. I think one of the reasons why I had been promoted to associate was that one of my colleagues had gotten married and my ex-husband and I went to the wedding.

Thelma: Was this a white woman?

Gayle: No, a black woman. We ended up at the table with the vice president and the dean and our husbands had some things in the common. So part of that kind of social interaction was that being there with the people who had some power in the tenure and promotion process, who have the opportunity to see you in a light that shows your talents, well it is to your advantage if you have aspirations to be in the academy. This probably helped me. You have to participate in the activities to rub the shoulders.

Thelma: So the social events are very important?

Gayle: Yes. The word came back to me that this was the point in time when the vice president began to notice just how bright I was suppose to be and how talented I was. So the folder was in front of her and she now knew me in a social context. Finally I got promoted. I think that's what probably happens but we just don't know it because we are not in the social contexts. We don't play golf with our colleagues, we don't go to Cape Cod, and we don't hang out at the club together. So I guess there is something to be said for those informal networks. If you are excluded from the golf course, and those informal networks are where people get familiar with one another, then the socializing doesn't happen.

My folder was solid but it was important for me to have that other contact. I figured out by the third or fourth year that just having a strong folder isn't all it's going to take to make it through the tenure process. There are other elements. As the Nancy Wilson song goes, I think it was Nancy, she spent her life exploring a "subtle whoring." It doesn't have to go all the way over to subtle whoring, but there is a social dynamic as well as an academic dynamic. There is the hard work you have to do, the day-to-day integrity that you have as a professional. But remember, human beings make these decisions. And these human beings operate on a lot of levels. It seems foolish to think that all of those levels are not operating. To some extent you have to able to play the game on all levels. Part of having gone to an HBCU for undergraduate school is the socialization process—learning how to operate in those arenas.

Inez: I have one African-American male colleague, and fortunately we like each other. For many of us the politics of singularity are that if there is another African American in your department, you may not have anything in common and you may not like them at all. There is an expectation on the part of your other colleagues that you should. It's a terrible thing because you don't and racism makes all things equal. Therefore you are in the same boat whether you like each other or not. So fortunately we like each other, thank God. It was fortunate also that he was senior, so he could chair my tenure committee. I owe a lot to him because he could read the signals. He knew how to read my institution.

Rachel: I want to share a story with you all that sort of ties together mentoring, collegiality, and racism. Just bear with me. Being on a search committee this year was very informative and one of the more painful experiences. One of the realizations was that in searching for candidates from all over the country, I learned that minority candidates sometimes got shafted. Let me explain how.

When we looked at their files, some had half-way decent publications, not in the top tier journals but somewhere just below. Some of them looked like they had solid teaching records and they presented their materials fairly well. When I read their recommendation letters, they did not compare to the letters that were coming from the same people for other candidates. White candidates were getting terrific letters; two- and three-page letters, creative in all kinds of ways. Our committee had a couple of minority candidates with very strong quantitative skills who had one-page letters with three paragraphs from the same people who had written pages and pages on white candidates. And I am not saying that every minority candidate deserves a three-page letter. I am saying that one of the things that I noticed was that there were less close relationships between minority candidates and their mentors, especially if their mentors were white. This is really disturbing because the minority candidates can't compete. They might have the skills that the white candidates have, but they can't compete.

The tone of the letters are much more hesitant praise than overwhelming. For example, "You would not be making a mistake by inviting this person into your department." The letters don't have that type of full endorsement of a candidate. This is disturbing to me because what this means is that in any national search, minority candidates get filtered into a very low-end pile. I am concerned about what that will mean for the discipline if people from the top programs are not able to get great letters from mentors. They won't be competitive in the top pile of applicants. They will always be in the special opportunities file. It's not where they want to be.

Thelma: Do you think it is solely because they haven't been able to foster a mentoring relationship in graduate school?

Rachel: I think it's because their mentors didn't foster those relationships. I think that white mentors with white mentees develop personal ties that enable them to develop a sense of that person's character. They have no hesitancy with regard to endorsing a white candidate on multiple levels because of this. With minority candidates, fewer social relationships take place—it is really more of an academic relationship. In addition, minority students frequently hide what they perceive to be their weaknesses from their mentors and monitor communication with them. I think all of those things contribute to poor relationship development, which impacts the letter of support. They don't want to overstate the case and write about what they don't know.

Thelma: I think that brings up an interesting point. One of the things that comes up in the literature in terms of faculty and the tenure process is that there is really this fourth category of the tenure process: collegiality. And it seems that if you don't participate or get together socially with people in the department and the faculty then . . .

Rachel: It's like one leg is missing and you're limping through the process.

Thelma: It is really coming through in the literature. That message is really coming through.

Rachel: And that is hard for minority candidates and faculty. It is a challenge to be able to socialize in a way that makes both faculty comfortable. For example, my way of communicating is much more casual and informal than my colleagues. But I didn't want them to mistake me as someone who can't or is unable to be a professional in my demeanor and in my career. I have cultivated a very professional persona. For example, I don't wear jeans to class. I try to respond to things in ways that are measured and conform to ways that my colleagues might hope young colleagues are like. It is important for them to see that they haven't made a mistake in hiring me.

I think there are other things, too. I sometimes say that when it is time for the Christmas party or the end-of-semester gathering, that is just more work for me. I have to know how to be socialized in their way. It's still being a professional while pretending to have a party. It is communicating in ways that make them comfortable and me uncomfortable. They watch people's behavior during meetings. Part of collegiality is to be pleasant even when I am angry. I try really hard to keep showing up even though my real feeling is I don't want to be around these folks. They disturb me.

Negotiating honesty is an issue also. How honest can I be and not ruin myself? For example, during the search process the decision was made to have a full committee meeting regarding a candidate who was a black woman. The faculty talked about her in some really bad ways. I was asked if I had anything to add, and I said that I thought this person was being punished for dong what emerging faculty were told to do. I don't understand it. She had published in graduate school, created articles from her dissertation, but they didn't value her research as important.

Someone came up to me afterward and told me that it was really brave of me to speak up. I wasn't thinking about bravery. I had just had it and they needed to know how I interpreted their actions. It probably wasn't the wisest thing to do because the people I directed my comments to have to decide my mini-tenure decision. But I don't care. I'm tired of it.

Gayle: I get tired too; tired of always fighting and walking on eggshells. But you can't get tired. I forgot to tell you all something about my experience with collegiality. I put the application in for promotion and the vote came back: One person voted for me and everyone else voted against me in my department. I wrote a letter asking for a meeting. This was getting to be a pattern—nonsupport from my department. When we met I recounted the whole experience of not having classes and having to struggle since I'd arrived. Finally the chair spoke up and said that the whole issue was that I was certainly talented but that I did not share my talents with the rest of my department.

Now remember, by this time I had discovered that I wasn't going to get any classes so I developed my own thing. I needed four classes, so I went to the general education department and started teaching an introductory research course. All faculty at my institution have to teach this course at least once. I had taught it so much that by the third or fourth time I taught it, the general education department asked me if I would coordinate all of the faculty scheduled to teach this course. So I became the faculty coordinator in a department outside of my home department.

In reality the chair was right, I didn't have a lot to do with my department. However, as I said at the meeting, I would have looked really strange trying to force my gifts on the people who had turned me away. Obviously, when I have no classes in the department, when opportunities for people in the department to showcase their talents have been given to others and not me, I do not understand how anyone could make a charge that I am not willing to work with people in the department.

I asked them to tell me something that people in the department have asked me to participate in that I have not participated. The chair said that she thought we would have bonded more at a summer program she sponsored. At that time my children were young. I participated in the program, taught my classes, and went home. As it was, the babysitter was getting half of my income. So I am not sure how this bonding was supposed to take place when I had external issues to care for as well.

Thelma: It appears that most of the collegiality issues center around service activities, yet service presumably should be focused on the least. Am I correct? What is the balance among teaching, research, and service on your campuses?

Jasmine: The distribution is about 50% teaching, about 35% research, and about 15% service. In my department, each of them has to be excellent. Mine is a university that gives the perception that it is a teaching institution and therefore teaching is the number one priority. The reality is that it is not, not in my department. I feel that my institution wants to be a research institution, but we are no where near having the funds and support that it takes to become a research institution. It just so happens that research is probably the area where I have not been the strongest.

Hope: At my school there is a commitment to teaching but I have to do other things. I have to have a research portfolio and I also have to show service. Those are the main three things: teaching, research, and service. There is a debate as to which is more important. It is supposed to be teaching and for all intents and purposes, I guess it is. Research and service are probably the least weighted. But research has been weighted more heavily in the past year.

Linda: If I had to put a numerical value on it, research is probably 60%–75%, teaching is 25%, and service is the rest.

Wilma: At my institution, it's teaching, scholarship, and service; that is the official policy, with teaching and scholarship as the primary criteria. Service is of less importance. But in spite of what they say, we know that even if you are a great teacher and your evaluations are off the charts, if you do not publish, you will not get tenure here.

Rachel: I know that in my department research matters most, and there is no question about that. I am convinced that the process is one that if you have the publications, the rest they'll fudge for you if they like you. If you have only teaching and service, they will not fudge the rest for you. Research is so crucial. At a research university that makes sense to me. Intellectually, I have understood that. I think what I didn't understand was how to make research happen. I didn't understand how to make research work and engage in it by trying to do all of these other things required for tenure. You have to make really hard decisions about your priorities, and I haven't made those decisions in a way that I am suppose to. For the second phase of the tenure process I need to demonstrate to the faculty that I can switch gears. I can reprioritize and put research first regardless of the commitments I have made around the campus that involve service and teaching.

Inez: Research is my institution's first priority. As long as you don't have any bad teaching evaluations you are fine. They don't care if they are mediocre or excellent. They only care that they are not bad. So teaching doesn't really count. Service, unless it is something extraordinary, doesn't count either. The institution likes to see that you are making progress or are recognized in your field. The fact that I was on program committees for national organizations and conferences was a plus. It showed that I was out there doing my work and that people in the discipline and beyond recognized me. That activity helps when it is time to get outside support letters from people in your field. But I have to say that if I didn't have any of these things it would not have mattered as long as I published. I really think anybody in a research university who thinks that anything matters other than research is being naïve.

Service and Mentoring

Thelma: I want to talk more about service. The literature reflects that women and faculty of color are asked to do more service than their white male counterparts. Are you asked to do more or different types of service than other faculty?

Wendy: Yeah, I do get over-picked. I was on several university-wide committees, but I am someone who likes to go out and work. My second year on campus I was asked to be on a high-level committee for diversity. This service really opened up doors for me around campus, but I ended up doing too much service. My dean told me that I did too much service. My thoughts were that some of the service the dean asked me to do and some of the service met my needs and fed me. I didn't know how I was supposed to choose.

I got a high-level administrator to agree to write a letter stating she recognized that because I was a black woman, I got asked to do far more service than other faculty. She agreed to do this if it came down to the fact that I was one publication short from other people in my peer group.

Eloise: I think in terms of service, the biggest challenges are self-imposed, as my challenges were not from the structure. It's difficult, though. I am a tenured full professor. I have a cushy job. Even now I say, "What else am I going to do?" Why did I need to be department chair? I needed to challenge myself.

Wilma: I did a lot of committee work as well. I was on every kind of committee. The school needed a token so it happened to me again and again. Interestingly enough, on those committees they wouldn't have listened to any advice I would have given no matter what I said. I can't imagine not having done it because there were so few black faculty in my institution. As an administrator, I recognize that black women get called on much more than others. I discourage my younger colleagues from doing too much service. I tell the new ones, "It's going to happen to you but I gave that, you don't have to give again." In other words, you will be over-asked but that is the institution's need, not yours. They need to say they had a black face and representation. So that's service you don't need to do.

Hope: I did a lot of my service on the department level. I did some on the school level. What I should have done was more on the university level. I don't think I did too much service. I didn't do the right type of service. I wasn't strategic about it.

Inez: Service has to be strategic and it has to serve the institution and the profession. It has to be strategic in the sense that it gives the institution something that it wants and needs. Outside of the institution it has to keep you connected to the core people in your field so they can write letters of support. You want people to say, "Not only have I read her file, I worked with her on the program committee of such and such conference or organization. This is what I think about her . . . " You don't have to do a lot service, you just have to do key things strategically.

Jasmine: My dean is relatively new. He created committees within our school, and one committee was for the recruitment and retention of students, staff, and faculty of color. I told you about this earlier. I was chair of the committee. He put two other African-American women, a Chinese faculty member, and a white male faculty member. The Chinese and the white male faculty members dropped off from the committee in the beginning due to convenient scheduling conflicts. The first thing the remaining people on the committee asked was, "Why did he put all of the people of color on the committee?" His reason was that it takes different techniques to recruit people of color and who would know those techniques better than people of color? I told him that I didn't want the school to see this as only "our" issue because we are the only ones on the committee. This is everybody's issue. He said that he would make certain that didn't happen. But he didn't force the other faculty members to stay on the committee.

Rachel: I have been on more committees for students of color than anyone in the department. I think in part because I was respectful of and helpful to those students interested in any issues having to do with race. And there aren't other people who are easy to work with and interested in race. On the other hand, the students are people who are different from the people in my department so it is a pleasure to find alternative visions of the university and the world. It helps me to stay sane. So I do those committee assignments in part for my own bit of "friendship network." I do them to let my department know that I have contacts all over the place and that this helps the department to present itself as a more diverse and well-rounded department. I am hoping that the service part of my tenure file looks really nice.

Linda: Women get stuck with particular types of service. My first year on campus I did more service than the law should allow. I worked with student orientation and talked to students generally. Students take up a lot of time being nurtured and getting help in class. I had to start coming in on weekends to do my other work and even then, when the kids found out that I was in on the weekends, they would come by. When you are going through this, you think that is how it is supposed to be. So much of what black students come to college for is to get help by black faculty. But students need to know that sometimes they are crippling us with their nonstop need to have that contact. Very few black faculty would be willing to give up all their contact with black students in the name of getting tenure. Some would, and do, but very few.

Thelma: Why do you think that most African-American professors would be unwilling to give up their contact with black students?

Linda: I think there is a sense of obligation. They didn't have black faculty to contact while in college so they feel they have to give what they didn't get to someone else. Or while in college, they had black faculty to contact who were very helpful and became their role model. In either situation it is a sense of giving back.

Thelma: But wait. It sounds like you are saying we shouldn't mentor our students. I hope I'm reading you wrong.

Linda: I am saying that unfortunately I think that sense of obligation is misguided—in the sense that the department doesn't structure the students, and they start to come whenever they want.

Rachel: I know what you mean, Linda. When you are in a department and you are the only black woman . . . the department has implicit expectations with regard to what students I might mentor, mainly students of color. I find out that I don't have anything in common with the student other than being a person of color. And if there is a promising minority undergraduate student, I hear about it from other faculty members, the implicit rationale being you should go talk to this person and encourage him or her along. It's not that these aren't fine things to do. It's just that other faculty are fully capable of the mentoring that would be helpful to these students. It's a double-edged sword because in some ways I want to be able to support students of color who are trying to do well. On the other hand, I want to do more of what my colleagues do, which is spend time on research and publishing.

I do mentor, probably much more than I should be doing for my own interests. It takes time to mentor. Students think, "I am the one person who is asking for this." In fact, it is five or six students asking for the same thing. I think it would be hard to avoid in some ways. I am learning that I have to start avoiding it. It is taking up too much time and I have these other things to do like my own research. Literally, they are not going to tenure me if I don't get more of my research out there. I won't be able to mentor anyone when I am gone. It is hard. For example, I am under a lot of pressure to read students' materials and I have a week. I have a week and a half to put together my own tenure file and turn it in. Right now it's only three inches thick.

Wilma: But we have to mentor. You have no control over people's attitudes. You have no control over the attitude of an administrator or department chair, but as a black women you do have control over yourself and your willingness and determination to be a mentor to someone else. You need to take some responsibility. Yes, people have a lot of work, the competition is thick. People have a lot of responsibilities, but that just has to be another one. Mentor somebody. Everybody should have a mentor and everybody should be one.

Inez: I mentor some but I don't mentor as much as I think I should within the institution. I don't think I take as much of a leadership role as I should. It is something that, now that I have tenure, I plan to change. I have people who I mentor outside. But I think my contribution to mentoring is a national conference that I chaired and helped to organize. I think that making that happen was my contribution to my peers and those that I teach. That is why I put so much of myself into it.

Thelma: How would you define mentoring?

Wendy: Mentoring is a combination of a little bit of guiding and being a resource to someone, like myself. A mentor lets me know what is pertinent information. It is about being honest even if it is being brutal. Telling me, "This isn't going to fly. I know you worked really hard on this but this is how it will be perceived." Also telling me what the critical things are that I need to look for, the pitfalls, so to speak. A mentor should call, be there when needed, and should be able to foresee what a need of mine might be and then fill that need. Now granted, not all mentors can do all of this.

A mentor should tell me when I need to go to a national conference. And if he or she can't go with me, then he or she should make some calls so that I have someone to hook up with and network with at the conference. Mentoring is done that way. I had people, nationally known in my field, take me under their wing and mentor me. When I submitted articles for journals, I had people help me coauthor, revise, and publish my work.

Jasmine: Mentoring is about really encouraging and supporting someone in doing their job. Being there for them, calling them, checking up on them, meeting with them on a consistent basis, finding out what is going on in their lives, asking "How can I help you? How can I be of service to you?" Really investing the time and energy involved in getting someone through the tenure process. To me it would make sense for every junior faculty of color to work together and mentor each other through the process. As a collective, we can get one or two people who have tenure to assist us and offer us advice. Mentoring is really about walking behind somebody and helping them along the way. If they stumble, pick them up, and say, "Okay, let's continue the journey"; but that hasn't occurred at my institution.

Hope: A mentor is someone you can confide in, someone who supports you. Not so much in a friendship fashion but someone who is a faculty member and knows what is going on because this person has been through the process or is at least ahead of you in the process. Mentors should show you how to get information and guide you through the significance of that information.

Wilma: Mentors try to give the benefit of the experiences, both positive and negative. Mentors have to be sensitive to the fact that someone else's experiences are never going to be the same as theirs. Mentors talk about what they have done and hopefully don't impose that advice. Mentors have to remember that they are dealing with other professionals and be sensitive to that reality. They also have to learn not to get hurt if people don't learn the lessons that they try to impart.

Try to remember one thing about mentoring: One never gets to give it back to those individuals who've mentored. One can only try to pass it on to somebody else. That is understood. Also, the responsibility to do outreach is on the mentor. That's why you pass it along. Those are values that I don't think are learned in the academy; you have to bring those values along with you. And don't obligate that person to owe you. The payback is, for example, when you see somebody else's book come out and you know that you have assisted that person. That is the reward.

Inez: I think I would only be interested in defining mentoring in the best possible sense. My definition is that a mentor is someone who tells you the truth, someone who actively encourages you to reach you highest potential. That type of active encouragement includes frank evaluation of your work. A mentor will tell you, "Well, you need to talk to X, Y, or Z. These are my colleagues who know about this topic." They provide practical, emotional, and intellectual support and they do not lie to you.

Rachel: Mentoring, good mentoring, is like an intimate relationship. It is a relationship with a person who has more experience with something than you do and who has had some successes that you haven't yet achieved. A mentor takes time to interact with you about professional issues and about some personal issues, around issues that matter to that discipline. This is a person who engages you in debates about your work, her work, and other people's work that are relevant to your discipline. This is a person who lets you know what the process will be like that you are getting ready to go through. A mentor gives you honest feedback about your whole self and everything that you have been doing. This is a person who finds a way to make sure she has read your work and gives you some suggestions on how to get it out there somehow. This is a person who shares experiences, knowledge, and compassion for what you are going through. This is a person who is willing and successful at engaging. I think mentoring needs to be about setting up mentees for making a good case for research.

Thelma: Did any of you have mentors?

Inez: Yes, less at my home institution. I think this is a crucial thing to say. I have learned the value of having mentors outside of my institution when I was a graduate student because I was the only black woman in the department. So the people that I turned to at that point were outside my department. They remain my mentors. I think it remains important for African-American women to know that mentors do not have to come from your home institution, particularly since we still find ourselves as the "only one" in our department. You have to have a range of people, both junior and senior, who know about the academy; people who can offer you very serious and frank advice. So that is key for me. If I was going to sit and wait for a mentor to come to my institution, I would still be waiting and I wouldn't have a job.

I have had several mentors. I have some friends who are senior in the academy who have been keeping an eye on my career, and all of them are critical to my development. Some were old teachers. I was in a very nurturing place as an undergraduate. I go back, even if I only go a couple of times a year. The mentors I had that really helped me succeed in this practice were outside and came in the form of teachers and colleagues who could read the institutional signs that I couldn't read. They would say, "No, that is not what they are doing to you. You have to get back on this." They were correct every time.

Eloise: I had a mentor who helped me develop from my master's degree to my doctorate. I also had mentors within my department but none of them were African American. They asked about publications and my career goals and then told me what I needed to know. Also, I got to meet key players in the field, but that was because the faculty at my institution knew them. They were really good at hooking me up with people at other colleges.

Hope: I haven't had any mentors. There have been some women in my department who were helpful, though. They gave me some information, but probably not about everything. There is one woman, a white woman. She was good at service. We both started at the same time so it was a peer situation. There were things going on in the department that I was not aware of and she would tell me about them.

There are a couple of things I want to mention. When I started and needed to do my tenure folder, a couple of people did offer me their binders and it was helpful, so I had an example. These weren't black women. The people at my institution are really nice, but in terms of giving me support and guiding me through this process, the "niceness" hasn't happened.

Linda: I wasn't mentored by anyone within my institution. I worked with people outside of the university.

Rachel: I think the support in my department has been light. Real support would be reducing teaching time a bit and providing some workshops around grants or research. I think that there has been a lot of lip service but no serious mentoring support for getting the research from the back-burner to the front.

There is a woman who has been really helpful about valuing my scholarship, in addition to the other things like my good teaching ideas, and so on. She has really been a person who has kept me sane throughout the process. She reminds me that while tenure is an extremely important process, it is not more important than me and my sanity. It is easy to forget that sometimes.

Thelma: Would you call her a mentor?

Rachel: Absolutely. She is my number-one mentor. I would have to say that according to my definition of what a mentor is, the white male in my department who helps me is also a wonderful mentor. These two people are really responsible for helping me finish my dissertation and get going on my research agenda. So I had two mentors: a white male and a black woman. Earlier in my career I had other mentors, but these two people are the ones helping me with the second stage; the post-dissertation stage.

Wilma: The woman who mentored me had gone through the tenure process and received tenure. So to that degree, I really did have an institutional mentor. She was an invaluable resource, but she was much more alienated than I was. The irony of it was that I was probably less alienated because she was already at the institution, yet there hadn't been anybody there for her when she arrived. This is why I am committed to working with other black women. What I wish I had had was a mentor in terms of my scholarship. There was no one doing the kind of work I was doing, so it took me a long time before I had someone to read my work and respond to it. The woman I spoke of earlier told me that I had to publish. If I had listened, I would have published more than I did. But you really have to have someone say that it would be great if you published that in journal X and help you do it. I have had unsuccessful mentoring experiences as well.

Thelma: Does it matter to any of you whether your mentor is a black woman?

Hope: I think there are gender and racial (or cultural) differences that I can talk to some people about, but not others. I don't think the other faculty members would understand. They don't understand the context. So I think it does matter whether your mentor is of the same race and gender.

Jasmine: It matters to me absolutely! When I first got to my campus, the institution tried to start a mentoring process. I was matched with a white woman and we had absolutely nothing in common. She didn't understand my needs at this institution. I was very uncomfortable talking to her. However, I can tell you right now that there is not one black faculty member who has helped me.

Wendy: I think it's nice to have that. I didn't have that. I had several mentors. One was a peer and we helped each other. My chair would look at my stuff and give me feedback. He would make sure I knew things about the field. He gave me opportunities. He was an associate editor of a journal in my field and said he wanted me to be a reviewer. He walked me through what it meant to review other people's articles. In terms of national mentors, they were women, but not black women. There were not many in my field; those who were worked in a different subdivision of the field.

I was pulled into a network (for lesbian women). There may have been some clique or homophobia going on in the other network I was originally in. It wasn't common knowledge that the new network was a lesbian network, but it was "common suspect." I was sort of vocal and they didn't like that. Most of them were still in the closet at their universities. All black women did not get pulled in, yet I was nationally known in another arena. As a result I couldn't tell why they wanted me to be part of this network. The "old girls network" was in operation. I became nationally known in my current field in less than five years, and it was because of that network.

Rachel: I think it depends on the person and the work they are doing. I think it depends on how the person grew up. I grew up in a community with other black folks. Not to be able to talk to other black people about the social process I was becoming involved in would have been difficult for me because the process was new and rather disconcerting at times. I need to be able to have someone to talk to about it, laugh about it, and be critical about it.

I think that as loving as my one white male mentor is, he has his own issues in the department with department politics. But his issues are not quite the same as mine. Mine have lots to do with racial and cultural patterns and how people interact. His gripes with the department are slightly different than my gripes. We are both confronted with the same old, white, male faculty that every department has; some of whom you think are really terrific and some of whom are really stuck in their ways, so to speak.

Wilma: I don't think it is required that your mentor be the same race or gender. I don't just mentor black women. I would have taken anyone in graduate school. I do think that as a black woman you have an obligation to mentor. I think we may speak to each other more personally. It's a political obligation, a cultural obligation; it is what you are supposed to do. Remember our earlier discussion. It's a payback for what was done to you. You don't mind that it is extra. I think it is generational. I think younger women have a different sense of their competition. They have a different sense that they can win that competition. Young people today are on the fast track and they have to be. They are much more assimilated.

Isolation

Thelma: A few of you spoke about what amounted to a sense of isolation as a result of the lack of collegiality and mentoring. Have any others felt a sense of isolation in your department?

Wilma: I've heard so many stories from other people about how isolating this process can be and I was never isolated. I'd go to a department meeting and I wasn't the only black person in the room. I wasn't the only black woman in the room.

Jasmine: I am the first one they have ever hired in my department, ever, and I remain the only one. I am not the only one in my school or on campus, there are a few. We do not talk together in a group. Interestingly enough, before I got here I received some literature from an organization on campus that would help mentor you. But when I got here it was mostly for black staff and very few faculty are involved. It is one of the loneliest and most isolating jobs I've ever had. I used to be here all the time, every weekend, working my butt off, by myself. I make an effort to get out and attend programs and if I didn't, since I don't have any family in the area, I'd be even more isolated.

Inez: I know what you mean. The worst part was the isolation and not having a lot of help, especially in writing. I don't think for most junior African-American scholars it is obvious how much help we don't get. When I look at the help my junior white male colleagues have . . . well, they might have continuing, very deep connections to their advisors, other colleagues, or people within their families who can help. They have other places to get help. And for many of us, we are the only person in our family who has ever done this. We don't have the same financial resources. I can't, for the whole summer, go to somewhere nice on the beach and write, so I think that makes it hard. One of the things that my colleagues talk about is that they see my car here at 8:00 a.m., seven days a week. And that was probably true for a while, a long time. I was here every day, plugging along. It was horrible, horrible. Do you have family support? Do you have friends? You have to have support. You have to have people who say to you, "This is exactly how you should be feeling right now. You're not crazy. Okay, maybe you are, but everybody feels crazy right about now."

Thelma: How are your relationships with the other African-American women on campus?

Jasmine: Remember that story I told you about the recruitment and retention committee meeting? Well, when the dean left, the two African-American women turned to me, jumped down my throat and said, "You were pretty quiet. Why didn't you have anything to say?" Mind you, these are women who walk down the hall and don't even speak. I said, "First, I haven't been here as long as you guys have so I don't have the history with this department that you have. And second, this is not the time and place for that discussion." They jumped on me because I didn't whine and moan about being placed on the committee. My point was that I didn't know what they were doing to help retain and support faculty. I told them that I am out there on campus and I make an effort. I am not going to let this department or this situation make me feel like I shouldn't try to contribute. I don't want that bitterness.

These women act like "been there, done that" and they don't want to be bothered. These are the same women who I have had to call out to on several occasions for not speaking when they walk down the hall. One of the women just got a Ph.D. a year and a half ago. And she's been at my institution for 20 years. That was an issue between her and the other faculty there. When she first got back from break, I congratulated her and would say hello to her, using her first name. She immediately corrected me in front of people and said, "It is Dr.!" My school is really big on that. Her office is two doors down from me. I asked her about her response and she told me that I had caught her off guard by saying hello. That was her excuse.

Thelma: Have any of the African-American women offered to help you with your tenure folders? For example, have they offered to give you their folder to use as an example or anything like that?

Hope: No black women helped me. No one really helped me. Some of that is my doing. I have probably had some opportunities.

Jasmine: No. One of the same women I just mentioned passed me the other night and asked me how things were going and how my packet was coming along. She didn't say, "Do you want me to look at it? Do you want my folder?" There was a person of color who was up for tenure who did ask everyone for files. The senior faculty members said they didn't have time to meet with that person.

Gayle: There is the expectation that someone might make some suggestions like, "You know we have to do this folder every year." I asked my two black colleagues if I could look at their folders so that I could have a model. Neither of them could produce a folder so I could actually see what one looked like. I have never seen any of their folders and I have been at my institution for 13 years. I did talk to my sister. I have a sister in the academy, and we have supported each other at every step of our careers.

Thelma: How have race, gender, and/or class played a role in your tenure process experiences?

Gayle: I think at the beginning almost all of it dealt with race. I don't think that department members were even aware that all of what they were doing was due to race. I got the job probably because of race, although I think the department got a bargain because they got a very qualified person. Part of the reason why people thought they could do and say what they said about me and my qualifications was because that works for most black people. The first thing the president and the union president said to me was that I didn't write well. They said that my publications weren't that strong. I write well—I was an English major in undergraduate school, so they had to take another look. Then the president made up the story about my service because the publications were solid.

Issues of race certainly seem to be implicated. I don't know that you can directly put your finger on it except that the language that people use with you and some of the assumptions behind what some of the people say seem to implicate race. Once a person spoke to me in a tone that I experienced as assuming I had "just walked through the door" as a new faculty member. I turned to the person and said, "This is my second year at this institution but I have been teaching for 20 years. And this is not my first college teaching experience. So what about me makes you think that you need to speak to me in that tone of voice?"

Rachel: This year, the bottom for me emotionally has been participating on the recruitment committee for another minority faculty member. It has been the hardest experience so far, as I shared earlier. The faculty has demonstrated an unconscious and conscious racism.

A black female candidate had done everything and was genuinely qualified. What happened was disturbing to me because I felt that this woman's record was turned around and upside down upon itself. A recent graduate, she created six publications from her dissertation. She had won awards and garnered support from people in her subfield, significant support. People wrote letters for her. She was rewritten as a failure. I watched that happen and it terrified me.

I was told that her training was inferior, she had no methodology, people said her presentation was incoherent. People said things about her that were impossible to believe. Her natural allies, the feminists in the department, turned their backs on her and destroyed her candidacy. As a result, watching that process was extremely frightening and painful for me. I felt that if they could turn her record upside down, they certainly could do the same to me. I genuinely felt that that is what happened in her case.

Thelma: Do you think that had to do with her race?

Rachel: Yes, it had to do with her race and because she had written about race. The perspective that was taken was that she wasn't writing within the discipline, that she had no methodology. People weren't as generous with her as they were with other young white scholars who had come to give talks to the department.

This was for a woman who is doing what they said they wanted. They want people to do as much as they can with their dissertation and then move on. She has done this very quickly, and usually people are rewarded for establishing a record of publication so quickly; they are seen as potential stars. And that is how people described her in their letters. What people can't understand is that it is really sophisticated, technical, difficult research. If someone who is a minority is doing something faculty can't understand, the minority candidate is suspect. So I was concerned by this.

Inez: I've experienced racism and sexism. No overt racism, but covert, yes. There was a lack of mentoring and a lack of explicit information about what I was supposed to do, how much was supposed to get done, on what level, where, when, and so on. At some schools they tell you that you have to have so many peer reviewed articles and when they need to be done. Here, nothing. Nobody ever said anything to me. No one was clear with me. The reason I know they were clear with other people is because I asked other people and they were clear. They knew more than I did and they were white. For example, I know two other people who came up for and got tenure when I did. All along the way they had more information. Somebody told them. I don't know if they had family, friendship, or collegial connections. But they had more information all along the way. They would tell me things I did not know and if I didn't keep up with them and ask them, I wouldn't have known.

That is part of the new racism. We treat everybody the same but if I am not in the informal network where information is transmitted then I don't know and I am not told. And those in power, senior colleagues, deans, and chairs don't perceive that as deliberate racism, deliberately or overtly denying me information. They just say, "that is how the system works. You find out information from your peers." Well if I am socially isolated at this school as an African-American woman and I don't have those networks, then somebody else should tell me. I think the whole process is permeated by racism. I think that my white colleagues knew that I and that people of color weren't, and still aren't, part of or included in those networks.

For my senior colleagues, part of their measure of whether or not you should be in "the club" [or network] with them is whether you can figure out that you aren't being included and that this is a game. If you can figure it out, then they are even more impressed. That proves to them that you are supposed to be there. If you can't figure it out, then their response is, "Well, she's a nice person" and "we weren't hiding anything." They will say also, "I didn't really know her. I tried to chat with her. She didn't quite seem to know the ropes and I thought that would change." They use this language to describe the new racism. And they can feel good about themselves and say that nothing was racist. It's the "fire in the belly" tactic. They say you don't have it and use it against you. They will think that if you had it, then you'd know what to do and how to get information about the process.

You have to be conscious and aware of all of the excuses. You have to be aware of the way the exclusion is manifested in your institution. Confront it and overcome it. If you sit by and think that simply doing your work will get you tenure, think again. It won't happen. How many African Americans do you know who don't get tenure and then people say, "But she was doing her work!" Doing one's work is not the only thing that has to be done. That's where the social reproduction part of the tenure process comes into play. New faculty need to remember that it is a way for tenured faculty to exclude folks from their ranks because they aren't like them. They have failed to master the social reproduction.

Eloise: Sure, I've experienced racism and sexism. I live it everyday. Maybe, that is just it. I go overboard and have the attitude that I won't be treated with a "slave mentality." I come in with that attitude, riled up sometimes, because I know it exists and can happen. I am prepared. I am always prepared.

Oftentimes people will come to you with racist remarks. You can bring it to their attention and help them see it. Their privileged status keeps them from seeing things. I don't care who it is, the dean, the provost, I don't care who it is. I challenge them there right on the spot.

One example was when I went up for a promotion and I had an external review just like everybody. The provost at the time said, "I think I want three more people's opinions." I wrote him a hot letter back. I said, "This seems like differential treatment. I know other people up for tenure and I am the only black and only female. Why I am I getting this?" They hadn't even said yes or no with regard to promotion. I just asked. I wanted to go on the record saying it looked like differential treatment because of race and gender. And I might be wrong. I will apologize if I am. But I'm just calling it like I see it. And after that, I did get my promotion. You have to call them on it. It smacks of racism. Tell me I am wrong.

Wendy: My tenure and promotion committee told me that I needed to do more discipline-based scholarship, and not the ethnic stuff, if I wanted to get tenure. I needed to work those networks in my discipline. When I got tenure I started doing more of the race and ethnic scholarship.

Race, gender, and class each had some impact. There was less of an impact with class. I knew how to talk the talk because I was raised middle class in a predominately white school system. I learned how to socialize, walk, and talk like they did.

Wilma: Another way that I am truly fortunate is that the freedom to do black studies was available to me. I taught courses on black women. Someone said, "A whole course on black women, are you sure there will be enough material?!" I assured them there would be enough. When I started, it was going to be a marginal thing, and that was fine. I had to have a sense of pride. I would be happy to work on the margins as long as I was free to do it. Who knew that it would grow to be this discourse that is so important to the profession? But when I started, the perception was that I could do that to begin with but that I was really smart and that I would go on to do something really important. But you persevere.

Jasmine: It comes from other faculty [with respect to race, class, and gender] and for me I can add another variable—age. There is an issue for some in the department when young black males come into my office. I had one faculty member stand in my office door and say, "How many of them have asked you on a date?" I said, "Not one. They came to see me for academic reasons just like all of the other students."

My first year here I was on a university-wide committee and we had a meeting in the library. I walked in and one of the faculty members assumed I was a student. He said, "Oh, this is a meeting for faculty. Students have to sit out there outside in the lobby area." He sort of flipped his hand out toward the lobby. I said, "No, I'm in the right place." We went around and introduced ourselves. When it was my turn and I said the department I was from, he apologized profusely. People do it all the time. And they talk to you so badly, so nasty. Then you tell them you are faculty and they change up on you. My point is that no one should be spoken to in that manner. I get it a lot. No one else in my department has to deal with that kind of crap; no one else.

Hope: As I told you, I had some problems but I am not sure how many of them were due to race or gender. Others suggested that the incidents may have been connected but I don't know. I never actually felt it. People have different perceptions. I think it's more difficult if you are a women who has other responsibilities like a family. There may be greater rewards for women who don't have the responsibility of a family.

Inez: I want to add something else. In my field, there are so few people of color. In that group of people, there are so few African Americans. I would say that my experience is that we are held to a different standard. We are seen differently as colleagues. With respect to race and gender, being an African-American woman is even more complicated. It is a gendered, racial perspective and it is a racialized, gendered perspective. We are a unique entity as black women and most of our colleagues don't know what to do with us.

I also think that when we talk about the subjects, if we talk about race, they are thinking, "Is that all you can talk about?"

When we don't talk about race, the question is, "Why don't you talk about race? You shouldn't be talking about the specialized subfield." It is an extra level of scrutiny. It's a hypervisibility and it's a kind of social isolation because people don't engage with us often. Frankly, I think it is incredibly difficult.

In my department a lot people have come who have some association with a graduate program that I attended. They formed sort of a club. But I am not a member of that club and some of my white colleagues are. Someone said to me yesterday, "Well I studied this" and then he mentioned someone's name and remarked, "But how would you know." I told him that I knew who he was referring to because I was in the same department. He doesn't even remember me being there. I think to myself, "Oh, okay. He can only remember me in some contexts and not in others." That is what I mean, it's a hypervisibility and yet it is a form of invisibility. It is such a complicated thing. It is a burden. It is a culture tax; a culture tax that we pay every single day. It's a tax that white faculty don't have to pay and I resent that. People come in here with the most mediocre kind of work and they present their work. The same work that if an African American or any person of color came in here with, they would be interrogated so much more and treated more severely. So I agree with what you said earlier, Rachel. They'll act as if the white colleague is a part of the family and that type of mediocrity is okay. The thought is, "We know he can do the work." Well, I went to the same institution with them and they don't even remember me. As a result, they don't know and won't vouch for my work. It is extremely complicated and difficult.

Thelma: Did you make decisions about scholarship or topics to teach because of this sense of hypervisibility?

Inez: Yes, in part because I understood this as part of my socialization in graduate school. It was clear that if I continued, if I took a dissertation topic about race then I would only be isolated. I would have been a marginal person doing a marginal subject. There are so few people who "do race" in my field. I had to do something they couldn't say anything about to have credibility and bring me closer to the center. I realized that I could be marginal socially, but I couldn't be marginal intellectually. It was simple. I knew it was the only way I could get the attention of the academy. Early on, I wrote some pieces that people thought were pretty political. I deliberately chose a dissertation that was a topic that could not be construed as a reflection of my ideology. It's what I needed to do to get straight into academe. Has my scholarship been influenced? No. People seem to like my work.

Thelma: Is that something you anticipated, which is why you didn't write about those topics?

Inez: I was older when I got my second graduate degree so I was smart enough to figure out how it worked. There were African Americans who came into that department who thought they could ignore some of the social issues. You really can't. It is hard for us to talk about this but we have to because the majority makes us face the issues. Find a way to face them on your own terms.

Rachel: I stopped talking about my research. The faculty makes me nervous because I study issues having to do with racism; these issues are close to the hearts of these folks. I know this based on comments that have been made during meetings. I think they know that someone like me would see some of their ideas as racist and as a result they don't know what to make of me. I think it makes them nervous. They don't know quite how radical I'd be. We just don't talk about my work. No one asks me about it, and I don't talk much about it, so it's one of those "don't ask, don't tell" situations.

It is not what I expected, but at the same time maybe I did. I am not sure. I have been doing everything for tenure but I think my research agenda is what is suffering the most. In part, maybe it has to do with confidence issues within me. Maybe the other areas are areas where I feel much more confident.

Before I got to my institution, I loved my research. Now, I still think it's wonderful stuff, but in my gut I am afraid of being penalized for it. I feel that it would be a real challenge for me to explain some of my intellectual perspectives to my colleagues and have them continue to respect me the way they do now, when they don't know very much about how I think about these issues. That is one of the big problems for me. There are not people with whom I can speak honestly about this issue. I don't know what is going on in the department or how it affects me, so I try to keep who I am and what I think very much under wraps. I am not willing to show who I am to these folks.

Inez: One of the things I would want to do in my own mentoring of African-American women in the academy is to help people realize what the new racism looks like. The new racism doesn't look like the old racism. No one in my department would make the social gaffe of making a racist remark in the open but they operate from racial assumptions. It looks very calm on the surface. But it is still racist and quite sexist.

People take the surface and the claim that things are okay. Because you get invited to people's homes and there are opportunities, it may be a long time before you realize how much you have been isolated from the critical goings-on in the department. And I think that operates with respect to race and gender. We have to talk to each other about how to read the new racism and how it works. In many ways it works like the old racism, but it doesn't look like it.

Thelma: In many ways I experienced that in my program and at work.

Inez: Yes, and you know what just happened to you. You're not crazy. I think it's a complicated and difficult time for African-American women to be in the academy. We have to know what to expect from the new racism. In my everyday life, I am the only one. Every single meeting, every collegial action, I am the only one. My tenure party was the most diverse party most had ever been to. That is because I brought all of my worlds together: my nuclear family, white women friends, the old guys, young people. They were amazed. Well, I live in a complex world. They are the ones that don't live in a complex world. But on a daily basis, my world is one where I am the only one; the only African-American woman.

Networking

Thelma: It seems networking might help to alleviate some of this isolation. Do any of you network on campus?

Wendy: There was a faculty member who made sure all of the black faculty got together for social things off campus. I tried to coordinate a "women supporting women" tenure and promotion committee where I would invite the senior women to talk to junior women about tenure and promotion. I did that my second year. I got ideas about strategizing to negotiate politics on campus from that network. For example, I learned how to organize my file, what committees were important, and so on.

Linda: No, I don't network on campus. There are colleagues in the department I talk to but nothing formal.

Wilma: From my experiences, I really had a sense of trying to be a mentor, particularly to other black women. A colleague of mine in another department has organized a black women's caucus, so we get together for social potluck dinners. The other part of the obligation we have to one another is to mentor women when they come on campus, especially those on the tenure track. It doesn't have to be a big group. But you have to have a core, otherwise people feel so lonely. We have had that experience in the department where people feel totally isolated.

Hope: There is one gradate student who I talk to on campus.

Thelma: Do you network outside of your home institution with other African-American women faculty?

Hope: I talk to my family. I also belong to some organizations, and I am active in some more than others. I do not network as much as I should, but more than I have in the past.

Rachel: I belong to national organizations. I haven't used them to network as much as I should. Creating networks requires you to call people. I am not as good at that, but I am learning to be better at it. Networking is controversial for me. I am not sure people always have time. And I am not sure who I want to connect myself to. I want to watch people and find out who they are before I say, "Let's get closer and share ideas about research." As a result, it has taken me a while.

Wilma: I know of a story that shows the importance of networking. There was one woman at my institution and she did everything! She published in the most prestigious journals. She didn't even get reappointment, let alone tenure. Her department was dysfunctional in so many other ways too, and so inhospitable. One of the things we tend to do is blame ourselves when there is a problem. This woman didn't share her experiences soon enough. It was because she thought her experiences were due to her failure. In fact, she could have used all kinds of reasons. She was given bad advice about what to do for tenure. Her promotion had been mishandled. When she did tell someone, we were on the phone chain. When you have a core support or network group, people watch out for each other.

There are other benefits to networking. In post-tenure you need to be able to have a productive life as a scholar. Mine has been very much affected by a network of "sista' colleagues" outside of my university. It is absolutely crucial to go to professional meetings and meetings with other black women who are doing similar kinds of work. I was tenured before I realized that people read each others work all of the time. I didn't want to show my work because I didn't think it was good enough. At conferences people were sharing work and getting that kind of critical feedback. That is how work gets done. It really does require both knowing other people and trusting other people. It is difficult to do any of those things if you are isolated. I go to conferences. Those are wonderful places to network.

Inez: Earlier I told you about a national conference which I chaired and helped to organize. That was a very dangerous move for me to make. It was highly visible. Afterward I, along with all of the black women from my institution who assisted with the conference, got called into our respective chairs' offices. Each of the respective chairs wanted to know how we were doing in terms of our research, our work, and our projects. In someway it was intended to be a positive thing but it turned out to have negative repercussions. They knew that we had become very visible and, as a result, the institution was going to be more visible. They knew that some of us were not on track. But we all felt that the spotlight had been turned against us. We ran that conference and we all taught our classes.

Frankly, I got very angry. It was said to me that I had done this conference and I hadn't done other things that I should have been doing. I didn't publish any long papers but I published several reviews that year. I applied for a grant, which I got. I thought I had a productive year in spite of that conference. That was a difficult situation.

The other thing I would say that goes to the importance of having mentors is that as a result of that conference, the senior African-American women who were my mentors recognized what this situation could become and wrote letters to the president of my institution. The letters told the president not to think about counting this situation against me and my colleagues. And they were very savvy about it. They said the work on the conference was to be considered as part of our scholarship. They wrote beautiful, very supportive letters. Nobody asked them to write those letters; that was very important. Their support made the difference because two of the letter writers were people the president knew and thought of very highly. And again, it wasn't something they were asked to do. To me, this was a golden expression of mentorship. And that helped to set a tone for me.

Rachel: I have a few friends who I talk to about what is going on, so I am not completely isolated. I think I have a network of three black women outside of the university who I talk to on a regular basis about what is going in my department. They are in my field, and one is a tenured faculty member. I met them through another experience I had. They have been really insightful because we talk about phenomena that are specific to black women, like the "institutional mammy." You go to a place and you end up serving, more than you do anything else, as we discussed earlier. At first when I came into the academy, I didn't think it would happen to me. I genuinely thought that I had a strong research agenda coming in and that I needed to learn how to teach. I thought that I was a little different. I am a different generation and I understand what is important in terms of the tenure process. And nevertheless, I now consider myself an institutional mammy; I have not broken the pattern.

Thelma: In what other ways have other women been a source of help, especially the three black women?

Rachel: One of the women, who is a senior member of my field, really values my research and my thinking on race issues. She thinks that what I have to say, and how I want to say it, is really smart. I think very highly of her work. Her work is very important to me and a number of other scholars of color, particularly women scholars of color. So for her to value my work and think that my work is important really matters right now, given that I don't even talk about it with my colleagues. I don't think they would value it very much. Some have, but it is a different thing. I have lost a lot of confidence. I don't know whether it is due to coming to this place or if it is the point in my career.

Eloise: I have a set of black women and, yes, family. There is one other black woman on campus. We talk and commiserate about things. They, the woman on campus and my family, have been my support mentors. There are two other women of color on campus, and we have been best friends since we walked on campus. We check in with each other, "Girl, did I read that right?" sort of thing.

There is a mentoring organization of discipline-based professionals and we meet once a year. We can use each other for external reviews. What happens many times is that we are not at a level in the ranks where we can help each other. So if any of them call me, I have to help them. I have to review their work because I am at the level of professor. It's not a rubber stamp (that doesn't help anything) but an early and consistent help. A level of mentoring that says, "Try this, try that." So that when they do go up for tenure, it's right. I have a girlfriend at another institution with whom I worked in that manner. By the time she came up for tenure, I had worked with her so much that I could write an effective external letter. Now she is a full professor with tenure. We have to do this. We have to network this way. It is critical that we have these reality checks. That is mentoring. We need to be able to ask someone who understands, "Did I read that right? Did I overreact? Underreact?" My sister will tell me this, blood and otherwise. I can't give myself a reality check. They will be honest and tell me.

Thelma: Why do you join these relationships?

Eloise: It's a pull. It's gravity. In the mentoring organization that I belong to, the other members' problems and concerns were similar to mine. There were both black women and men there, too. I have tons of colleagues that I respect. I don't have many friends. At those functions I can have the academic challenge and the social side addressed as well. It's only natural, I think, as I am from a black town, black high school, and a black college. When you get to an institution where you feel isolated, you gravitate toward making the connection.

However, I understand why I am at my institution. I wanted that isolation so I could do my work and research. It was a deliberate act for me to be at my institution. As a result, I have to be deliberate in making networks and connections.

I have to stay grounded and focused. I am in a sorority. I go to family reunions. I have to see the people who really mentored me and made me the person I am today. I take no credit. I was lifted up by my family. They gave me my focus. I had a chance to go to an all-white college, but my parents wanted me to say grounded and focused; they knew what I needed. It is because of this that when I got to this institution, I knew who I was and there was nothing folks here could do to shake me, take away my confidence or sense of self. It is not going to be diminished by someone asking me, "Are you sure you are good enough?"

Jasmine: I don't network really. There were two black women with whom I spoke. Ironically, they teach at black colleges and they gave me some advice but it was a one-shot deal.

Gayle: One of the things that my sister (who is in the academy as well) and I spent time doing, both collectively and individually, is thinking about our academic philosophical position, our philosophy of living. That is probably metaphoric for the fact that you have to stake out a position and stick with it. If you don't have a position, you could be anywhere: philosophically, academically, and theoretically. Part of this whole process is, "What does it take to make me function and be happy?" When it's all said and done, I derive great pleasure and satisfaction from what I do. I really like what I do.

Highlights and Lessons Learned

Thelma: Have there been any highlights during your respective processes?

Inez: A great experience in the tenure process was to be on sabbatical and to find other intellectuals with whom I could really talk to about my work and be appreciated for my insight. Without that I would have been up in the air and isolated. That year was good for me. It also pushed me to do better.

Linda: I had to meet with the college-level tenure committee. I had had a positive meeting with the department, but the college level had no idea what I was writing about or why I was doing the research I was doing. This was because of issues of competency on their part. The meeting was a great thing. I was scared because the outcome of the meeting was going to determine the outcome of their vote. Had they already voted, it would have been overwhelmingly unfavorable. But because they weren't sure, they invited me to talk to the committee and discuss certain aspects of my research. This was a good thing because sometimes they don't want to see you.

I sensed a lot of embarrassment on their part. We got into a long conversation, and so many of the things I was talking about they did not know. I knew their theories. But because I wasn't using their theories in my work, they assumed that I did not know them. Because had I known them, I would have certainly thought that those were the best of all possible theories to use. I went in feeling nervous and left feeling sad because I had colleagues who were in the position of making decisions but they knew so little. They had depth but had so little breadth.

Rachel: I got a teaching fellowship. It was a very prestigious award on campus.

Jasmine: I was told last year that I had a really good chance of getting tenure. My department chair said that he was 99% sure I would get tenure. My service was really good. I had to focus more on research. The chair and the new dean told me I was on track for tenure but as far as promotion, they want to see more research; which in the end is really interesting. I have had five grants since I have been at my institution, but in my department publishing outweighs grants. I was told to cut down on service and I did. Ironically, this year I got an award from my school for service. We have awards for teaching, research, and service for faculty and one of my faculty members nominated me for my service. That is where my heart is, in teaching and service. If I had wanted to do a lot of research, I would have gone to a research institution.

Thelma: There seem to be few highlights. Why do you stay?

Jasmine: Because of the students. I have resolved the fact that it is difficult to get support from the faculty at my institution. I have struggled and dealt with it. There is no cohesion. The most senior black faculty member has only given me one piece of advice since I got here. He said, "You have to find something and make it your baby." That is what I did and that is how you survive. That has been a hard pill for me to swallow, the lack of support from black folks.

Thelma: If you had to go through tenure again, would you?

Jasmine: No. I have a problem with the entire process. You're being evaluated by faculty who aren't in your discipline. The disciplines are so different. They don't know what the top journals are. I am seeing more and more that it is becoming a "brag fest" and how much you can talk about yourself. You find out those kinds of things the hard way. You'll fall on your face before someone will tell you.

Hope: With the hindsight that I have now, I would do the process again, but I would do things differently. I would hassle people to death. I would get information. If it were the same time of my life, I would try to do more scholarship early on.

Rachel: I probably would. I fit the academy better than I thought I would. I want to change the academy, at least my discipline. I'd do it again but I say this with some concerns about what it says about me. I would put more emphasis on research early on.

Thelma: Do you have any words of advice or lessons learned that may help new African-American women faculty members successfully negotiate the road to tenure?

Jasmine: When you go to conferences, sometimes you have to pay for it with your own money. One thing that I do when

I write a grant is to write travel into my application. I also write in my release time because it takes time to work on a project. Another thing I have learned is that it is very hard to do research by myself. Get your research agenda together right away, as soon as you step on campus, if not before. It's really hard to find support, but you have to get it from someone. It might even be a staff member on campus. Or you might have to get someone outside of the university to help you. If there is something you are experiencing that isn't right, get people behind you and have them help you get over the hurdle. I think it can be done. There is a place for you and you are needed. Tough it out because the students need you. It will be a challenge. I always hear it's a challenge anywhere you go.

Wendy: I knew what I wanted to do when I came to the university. I knew I wanted to be nationally known in less than five years, so I plotted it out. You have to play that game. If the institution wants me to jump through a hoop, I'll jump through that hoop. I'll talk big after I get tenure.

You have the ability to do this. It is about pushing on. It's about learning what to do politically to put yourself in the best position. You have to play the game when you can. Keep your ethics, but play the game. Get on a committee that has wide appeal or wide support from the college. Also get something that feeds you, gets you involved on a national level. Think about the tenure process early on so you wouldn't get freaked out by all of the work that has to be done.

Also know that whatever you feel is real. It is real. Black women have to know it is going to be okay. It is a process that basically validates what you already know about yourself. It's a process where people on the outside are determining whether they want to take you on for life. I had the attitude that I can stay or I can go. I was clear that if I left, I was going to go at the third-year mark or earlier because leaving after that it would give the indication to people that I was leaving to avoid tenure. So if you are thinking about going some place, think about going in your second year. That is why I applied for another job in my second year. I didn't know if I wanted to go anywhere but I was prepared to leave if necessary.

Hope: Get to know many people across campus, not just in your discipline. Become more assertive, not a pest, but more assertive. Talk to people about their projects and about their portfolios. Ask them what they are experiencing in the process. It is better to know what the important areas are and choose whether to face them. It's political no matter what you do. If things come up that are really strange, document them. Also, do not teach the same courses all of the time. I have added an additional course so I am not teaching the same courses over and over. I was told late in the process that I should have done this before. Now we have a new chair, and he is more supportive.

Wilma: I would say there are three components: teaching, research, and service. The most important of these is scholarship or research. I would tell her that I know she wants to be a good teacher but that she has to put her primary efforts in scholarship. Once the dissertation is finished, part of that work can be extracted and sent out as an article. Also, she has to be collegial.

The way to compete in this environment is that you have to find a way to get a fellowship and identify it early. Find a way to get some time off so you can have extended time to write. I am not comfortable with the weighting; teaching should be weighted much more than it is. I will tell her that you will be called on to do more service than you need to do.

Also, you can really get turned around by what other people say about you. You can't give people that kind of power. The thing to do is to keep on doing what you think you are called to do. Writing can be very isolating, very lonely, very hard work. I would have found a way to have gotten more of my ideas on paper earlier. I would have shown them to someone else earlier. Oh yes, if there's a choice between writing a conference paper or writing an article, write the article.

Eloise: I had seen some journals and I thought I could review for them. So I took it upon myself to contact the directors of publication for the journals that had calls out for reviewers. They started sending me articles to review. As a reviewer, I started sending back very thoughtful and deliberate comments and ideas, and the journal would say that I should write my comments as articles. Later, I was asked to be on the editorial board; then I got to be the chair of the journal. It was because of the fact that I was curious about how journals worked. I also wrote to international journals. I had an international reputation before I had a national one.

When developing your research agenda, think about what you are really passionate about and what it is you want to know. If you are passionate, then you know you are on the right track. Know both qualitative and quantitative theories. I tell new faculty that they have to do things to take them into other venues. Your writing will be analyzed by external reviewers who have different theories. It's something you have to go through in the tenure process. If you are grounded in a philosophy and a theory that stems from your core beliefs and philosophies, you can't be shaken to the core every time someone questions you. Make sure you can defend your work, your theory, your philosophical world view.

I don't know where that level of confidence comes from but you have to bring it with you. Tenure is a tough situation to negotiate or navigate. The tenure process is inherently hierarchical and oppressive. Being black and being a woman, I understand hierarchy and oppression quite well. I tell people to keep their confidence. People will try to make you less than you are and confidence is the key. I am a team player. I will always be a team player. But I cannot let anybody minimize me or define me. You have to define yourself. It was a hard thing to think about but I always kept it in the back of my mind. If I said no to a dean or a colleague, I would have to be prepared to take the consequences, whatever they were. If it meant not being tenured, then fine. The college down the street could use me. I have confidence that what I know and what the world needs to know dovetail one another. Be clear and call it what it is early on. This is key. I know my field well. I would tell a new faculty member to learn all she can learn so she doesn't have to "back door" anything. Walk boldly through the front door.

Inez: There are things I would do differently. I would be more conscious of things in the process. There is way too much stress. We, as African-American women, talk about it but don't deal with it. I would have more friendship networks that cross over into professional networks; someone to hang out with but who will also say, "Girl, you need to read and stay on the edge of what is going on." I would tell the new faculty member to have a friend who will find you and check on you. I have a friend who, when she was writing a book, had a person that she talked to two times a day. Just to check in. I have a network. I tell them, "Criticize me now. Tell me now." Criticizing now is better than screwing up in the street later. I wish I knew this before. I don't know why we as African-American women don't talk about that. We'll talk about Michael Jordan or the new Oprah movie, but how often do we get together to talk about our work in a social setting? It is very a odd thing but we need to do it.

I would tell a new faculty member to be aware and find out what the institution wants from you and when they want it. Don't stop until you get very specific answers. I think that knowing to ask for help is okay, but knowing who to ask for help is key.

You have to have senior mentors, senior faculty outside the institution you can count on to give you support. These should be women who will give you information about your work in time for you to do something about it. I would tell her not to hold her manuscript back. Find out who in your field can read your work. Show them and don't wait until right before tenure to show it to them. Ask all along the way, "How can this be improved? What do I need to do?" Ask for concrete examples. By the time the department gets your work, it's polished and it's good. There are no gaping holes intellectually. It could be someone you went to graduate school with who is a very good reader.

Then you need people who can help you position yourself professionally. Go to conferences. You don't have to go every year. Ask the department how many and what type of papers you should do. Ask how much time you have to establish a good research record. Have someone help you lay out your research plan and your other work.

Rachel: If I had to give a new faculty member a few tips, I would tell her to take whatever she is working on and create some articles out of it immediately. Try to write relatively short pieces and send them out right away; the best she can create in five months and send the papers out to the top journals. I would encourage her to do that on a regular basis year after year. The goal would be every year to send out three or four items so that every year she is getting feedback on her work and she is getting a sense on how to get it out there. Beyond that, make sure to let the chair know "no extras." No extra committee work, because these are your years to work on publications.

I would say that the first three years should be spent establishing a foundation in research instead of teaching. The second three years should be spent increasing your research and then building a service record and more of a teaching record. So I would tell the person to do public presentations of their work among peers. For the first three years, have a minimum of $800 set aside for going to meetings and conferences.

I think it is not a very carefully crafted process. The big question for me is, "Why haven't I been able to do this for myself?" Part of it is that I've just discovered how important all of this is in the tenure process. I understood at a theoretical level before. I understand now at a more personal level how important it would have been to do this.

Gayle: Take every opportunity to showcase yourself. You have to be prepared to take advantage of the opportunities because, if you are going to get one, you may not get but a little bit of a crack to slip through. If you don't have the skills to go in and capitalize on it, then not only may the crack close but it may never open again, for you or anybody else. You have to know what you are talking about and you have to be good at what you do.

Thelma: Do you think she should find a mentor?

Gayle: I think she should. Everyone needs a mentor inside the group. But she also needs to have a network. I agree with Inez.

I have been very direct with people. The pattern is stuff happens, I give myself time to think about it, and then I write a letter. I write something about it because I create a record. Part of the strategy for me was to make a determination that I was going to be at my institution, that I was not going to be frightened, self-conscious, or feel backed up into a corner.

You may want to assume that potential treachery, and think about what is the best way to deal with that potential treachery. It helps to have a sista' friend on the outside. You need a mentor and you really need a strong advocate; someone who really wants you to be there. Someone who will tell you the little things you need to get to succeed, such as having a computer and a little copier for your home office. I didn't know just how helpful those things would be.

Linda: One of the things I found was that I was often being reviewed by people who did not have a grasp on my discipline. This often happens, especially with relatively "new" disciplines such as women's studies, African studies, and ethnic studies of any kind. Being evaluated by people who don't understand what you are doing is hard, but being evaluated by people who are hostile to what you are doing is one of the most difficult parts of the process. It makes you think you're not very smart. It makes you wonder how you got where you are. I soon discovered that some people get where they are by controlling the reward system or the reward structure and even the competencies.

Thelma: Any closing remarks?

Wilma: Absolutely. This is a privileged life. It is absolutely a privileged life.

Gayle: It is a great job. Listen, anybody who tells you differently that teaching at a college and being a full professor isn't the best job on the planet, well they are wrong. They are wrong. I make as much money as I have time to go make. I don't mean that I make all the money in the world. But, we are sitting here on a Friday and I don't have anywhere to go. I didn't have anywhere to go yesterday. I don't have anywhere to go most Tuesdays. I may have to go somewhere on a Saturday, but I don't HAVE to go if I don't want to. My base salary is not dependent upon any of these extra things I do.

Teaching is a service profession. I expect to have to serve the students but I don't expect to have to work really hard to have collegial relationships or any relationship. The mistake that can be made is that you start fighting the people in your department. Decide what you want to do and confront the issue. Look and see if there is some way you can accommodate what they need from you and still keep your integrity. But have some level of recognition that you're going to conquer this. The tenure process, as flawed as it is, is one that probably does have some rationale to it. Certainly, it's like any political process, ripe for corruption, and I am sure it is corrupt. However, any other system that you come up with will likely have the same opportunity to be corrupt.

Rachel: My task is to be intact no matter which way this process goes and that is tough. Part of me is saying if I don't get tenure at my institution, which isn't even the high-end place that I came from, then this really is a scary process and I failed it. I would like for things to go well. On the other hand, some of it is beyond my control and I need to let it go. The parts that are in my control I need to work on and fix before it's just too late.

I view mini-tenure now . . . I can use it for many purposes. If the faculty members like me, but don't see much potential in me, it is a good time for them to say so. At first I thought that my reappointment was a given . . . but since I have not completed my book manuscript, I can only put a few chapters in [my portfolio]. The worse case scenario is that they don't reappoint me and I'll get another year to find a job. They can decide that there isn't enough scholarship and they don't expect there to be enough in three years. They want to save themselves the trouble of having to go through tenure with me. In many ways I don't think this will happen because I have a strong teaching and service record. And I think the department can begin to see the potential in research. On the other hand, if the people who are on the committees decide they really don't want me around, it is the perfect time to get rid of me. They can definitely justify it by a lack of research on my part. I haven't written for grants or anything like that. It really depends on their mood. It depends what the climate will bear. My department is trying to increase their rank, so they are trying to decide how the younger people will participate and get tenure. Plus, post-tenure review conversations are happening. It becomes a more significant issue about who gets tenure and who doesn't. They are no longer willing to invest in people they think aren't worthy. I don't like being judged differently than people who are already in the department.

The real issue is to recognize that this decision-making process is a thing separate from me. I have to keep reminding myself that there is going to be a "me" whether or not there is going to be a job with tenure for me. My black female mentor is the one who has continued to remind me of that. She said, "Look, you're going to be a great scholar whether this place chooses to recognize you or not. You have the skills." That's been a struggle and I know it will be a struggle for me until the time comes.

Gayle: You do struggle. Like you, Rachel, I didn't know where this process was going to go. I thought that if I could handle the worst thing that may happen, then go for it. If I can't, then leave it alone. I was watching Oprah one day during the time when she was going through her trial. I heard someone say, "There is no need sitting around thinking that you can't believe this is happening." It's happening, deal with it. I think that that is a real good message. Part of it is you are who you are. Part of it is you created this. You decided that you wanted to be in the tenure racket and this is the way the racket works. The one I went through was more transparent than a lot of systems. Usually people don't know how the decision is being made. At this institution most of the racket is right out there. At least if you know what it is, you can learn how to fight it.

Thelma: Thank you, ladies. I've learned a great deal from each of you.

The Game of Tenure 5

This chapter analyzes and synthesizes the rich data set. It identifies the benefits and rewards of tenure from the perspectives of the women interviewed. It details the difficulties and negative experiences encountered as they moved through the tenure process, including figuring out the rules of the game, balancing roles and responsibilities, and finding supportive colleagues and mentors. It then offers 12 guiding principles to help African-American women successfully negotiate the tenure process, develop collegial relationships and mentors, and find one's stride and balance among research, teaching, and service.

The nine black women faculty members tell fascinating stories. Their individual stories, when woven together as in the roundtable, create an intricate discussion of both the pitfalls and the promises of the tenure process in academic institutions. When viewed closely, this discussion can be formatted neatly into a career guide for any new faculty member. However, these guidelines are especially true for African-American women faculty.

For those who have been awarded tenure, the women agreed that although they had had several negative experiences, in hindsight, they would participate in the process again. They thought that the rewards of tenure were worthwhile. Once tenured, the rewards were likely to include relatively high salaries, favorable work schedules, and job security. The women "fit" into academia—they were comfortable in their institutions (once tenured) and able to continue challenging themselves by taking on administrative positions. They led conferences and mentored other black women faculty and students. They also enjoyed being scholars, as they had the ability to contribute their thoughts and ideas to the discipline with the hopes of providing a new voice to the literature.

In spite of these things, the negative experiences seemed to overshadow the positive ones. Discovering that the tenure process was "a game to be mastered" was the leading cause of hardship for the participants. Once discovered, however, the women decided that they would play the tenure game as *informed* participants. And although they could not control the actions of others (e.g., colleagues, department chairs, and deans), each woman simply readjusted her tenure-based activities in order to make the process more bearable.

Only one of the participants, Jasmine, stated that she would not take on the tenure process again if given a choice. She stated that there were too many negative aspects and in hindsight would simply opt out of the process.

There are various points at which these participants experienced difficulties. Most of the difficulties occurred around four particular issues: 1) learning the rules of the game; 2) negotiating the balance among teaching, research, and service (and life outside of work); 3) collegiality; and 4) finding a mentor. Racism and sexism permeated each of these issues.

Learning the Rules of the Tenure Game

All the women either explicitly or implicitly recognized the tenure process as a game of sorts. There are rules to the game, both written and unwritten, spoken and unspoken. Each participant acknowledged that they received an official written document on the requirements of tenure that was vague and general at best. Five of the women had no contact with their department chair or dean regarding departmental or college-specific requirements for tenure prior to their third year in the process. Of the remaining four participants who did have contact prior to year three, one approached the chair and initiated the conversation. A second stated that her conversation with her dean was general, unhelpful, and filled with negative statements about what "was not required" for tenure.

For each participant the process of tenure and promotion was bifurcated; in other words, tenure and promotion was decided separately. There were different application processes and oftentimes the decisions were made by different committees. But again, there were no conversations about specific requirements, timeframes, or presentation formats.

Each participant had a yearly departmental review. However, it should be noted that although the reviews were used in the tenure process, none of the participants were informed of this by their department chairperson or dean prior to the first or, in some cases, second annual review.

These annual reviews provided opportunities for the faculty to set agendas (for teaching, research, and service goals) and later be assessed based on whether they were able to meet those goals. At year three, the process became more involved; some referred to the process as "mini-tenure" or "third-year review." There was some acknowledgement on behalf of the participants that in this year the stakes were higher and the review was to be more intense than years prior. Two participants had to get outside letters from colleagues in the field to attest to their value to the discipline. Two others had to have books for mini-tenure, although it was not clear whether they needed book contracts in hand or completed manuscripts.

Each of these women stressed the importance of learning the rules very early in the tenure process. It was clear that learning the rules in the second or third year of the process was entirely too late. Clearly, this can be seen in Rachel's comment about learning and mastering the tenure game simultaneously. To have done otherwise would have led to a stressful and detrimental six years for Rachel at her home institution.

The participants' experiences were not unlike the findings highlighted in the literature. The women participated in a six- to seven-year process of earning tenure. For the most part, as African-American women, they were aware of the formal or written rules for tenure and unaware of the less formal or unwritten rules. Inherent in the literature, however, was the idea that new faculty were given detailed information about the tenure process at the start of their careers. For the majority of the participants in this study, that was not the case, leaving the women to fend for themselves in the critical, early years of the process. This in itself is problematic in that the participants were expected to perform early and often without knowing the "real" guidelines and requirements from the start.

Also, it appears this was more of a problem for the participants who more recently entered the academy as faculty. For both Eloise and Wilma, the more senior of the group, guidance and feedback began almost immediately upon stepping foot on campus. From the data it seems as if 20 years ago, when there were fewer black women faculty in the academy, there was a formal effort made on behalf of academic institutions to assist these women through the process in order to increase the number of women and minorities at institutions of higher education. In more recent years, there seems to be less of an emphasis on assisting black women faculty through the process. In many of the later cases, the participants were the only, or just one of a few, black women faculty on campus.

Negotiating the Balance Among Teaching, Research, and Service

The data indicates that among teaching, research, and service activities, research is the primary factor influencing the tenure process. Service and collegiality, together, are a strong second, with teaching a strong third or fourth. However, it was not necessarily the quality or quantity of the activities that mattered: it was the "type" of activities performed by the women. The teaching, research, and service had to be of a particular genre in order to be accepted by mainstream traditional faculty within their respective institutions.

The women stated that their teaching activities varied. Each recognized at some point in the process that they should not teach the same courses semester after semester. Once recognized, each negotiated this issue differently. The majority developed new courses or taught interdisciplinary courses in other departments to broaden their teaching profile and expertise.

Seven of the participants made decisions about whether to teach and research "minority issues" solely based on whether such topics were of interest to them. (The two remaining participants did not think about a teaching or research agenda, thus it was not an issue for them.) They recognized, however, that their work could be perceived as marginal and some were willing to accept this as a drawback. Inez was one of these women. She said that her scholarship has not been influenced by her race and gender. However, the data suggests otherwise. She made deliberate choices *not* to write about race and gender initially because she knew that she could not afford to be perceived as marginal intellectually. The inference here is that Inez may have wanted to write about issues pertaining to race and gender but she knew, pre-tenure, that her ideas would be seen by the academy as marginal and thus unacceptable.

All of the participants wished that they had implemented their research agendas earlier in their career. Six participants began their faculty positions by trying to establish themselves as good teachers so they put their research on hold. All of these women acknowledge that this was a mistake. Research, regardless of institutional type, should be the first priority. And while service cannot and should not be avoided, they suggested it should be done strategically.

All of the women commented that initially there was no method to the service activities in which they participated. It was not until their third year or later when most discovered that the service needed to be *strategic* service. Strategic service can be described as service which makes the faculty member known on (and off) campus, within her field, and that which is selected to advance the career of the faculty member without interfering with research.

The women also agreed that it was necessary to be a mentor to other African-American women faculty (and to students) as part of their service activity. However, there was some disagreement as to when, and to what extent, this mentoring should take place. The more senior faculty agreed that mentoring should take place once the research agenda had been established and was well underway, perhaps as late as after the awarding of tenure. The junior faculty suggested that it should and for them it did, start much earlier.

Again, the difficulties of the participants in prioritizing and balancing their roles as academics were similar to the literature. The participants were frequently asked to be the "minority voice" on committees and in other service opportunities. They were more likely to teach marginalized courses and courses relating to the "minority experience" within the particular disciplines. For the majority of the participants, their research suffered because they were placing more focus on teaching and service, thus delaying the implementation of a research agenda. On a positive note, several of these women consciously broadened their teaching portfolios and began to select service commitments more strategically as time went on.

Collegiality as the Fourth Category of the Tenure Process

Collegiality was an enormous issue for all participants. They each acknowledged that there was a social aspect to being a faculty member that, while uncomfortable at times, could not be avoided and was essential to moving through the tenure process. Each felt as if the collegial aspect of the tenure process put them in an interesting dilemma. The participants felt forced to foster relationships with other faculty members in their department. Often, they had to take the initiative to start and cement the relationship, while there was a perception that colleagues were often unavailable or unwilling to reciprocate the effort.

To these women, collegiality was about more than saying "Good morning" and other simple pleasantries. Collegiality was about being perceived as a team player, attending social functions sponsored by the department or institution, sharing "talents" with the department, and assisting colleagues with projects. These activities were problematic for the participants because it forced them into situations where they had to negotiate honesty and integrity, with the fear of being penalized for making the "wrong" decision; that is, choosing honesty and speaking out against an injustice or unfair situation as opposed to being perceived as a team player and keeping one's mouth shut.

There were several such instances when the participants were put into situations where there was an imbalance of power. Specifically, the participants found that they felt compelled to participate in "pet" projects of department chairs and senior faculty members, with all parties knowing that such activities would take time away from the participant's research activities. There was a fear of reprisal if they refused the "opportunity," as these senior colleagues were the very ones who would evaluate them and play a direct role in the tenure decisions (as most tenure and promotion committees are made up of full and associate faculty who have earned tenure).

Participants also found that there was an expectation that they would participate in social activities such as holiday parties, events sponsored by the department, weddings, and other events. These events placed an extra level of work on the participants because they knew that if they failed to attend, it could be perceived as noncollegial or an open rejection of departmental norms. In other words, the perception of the message being sent by the black woman faculty member was, "I don't want to play with you." But the real message was, "Playing with you really isn't playing at all. For me it's more like pretending to play in order to prove that you should let me stay on the playground."

However, when it worked, it worked. Gayle told a story about how collegiality benefited her at a crucial moment in the process. Attending a social function allowed certain decision-makers to get a better look at her and gauge her demeanor and ability to be collegial. This helped in the long run because the individuals involved remembered Gayle when it came time to reevaluate her application for promotion.

The participants experienced collegiality much as it exists in the literature. They found that this unwritten "fourth category" could both help and harm their bid for tenure. They also experienced collegiality, as Gayle so eloquently stated, as a "subtle form of whoring." In other words, the majority of the participants had to put themselves out to colleagues as receptive to engaging in team and department work. They were trying to prove themselves as scholars and good team players. It was similar to standing on a corner with a sign that read, "Look at me, I'm collegial and I'm good at what I do!" In each of the participants' cases, what was different was that there were no handwritten placards, merely efforts to successfully balance teaching, research, service, and all of the extras.

Finding a Mentor

Each participant agreed that it is necessary to have a mentor and to be a mentor. They agreed on the necessity of having at least two mentors: one within the institution (preferably within the department) and one outside of the institution and within the field. While each agreed that the best case scenario would be to have a mentor who is an African-American woman, only six participants said it was a must.

Although most stated that they would have accepted a mentor of any racial or gender group, the participants identified some qualities an ideal mentor should have in order to help negotiate the road to tenure. An ideal mentor would be in the same field or subfield as the mentee. The latter was not a requirement, but an ideal. Having a mentor of any sort would have been beneficial, but having a black woman mentor is akin to having a mentor who is within the same discipline-based, specialized subfield. In the former situation, the mentee has the opportunity to learn the inner workings of the discipline. In the latter, the mentee has someone who can "school" her to the inner workings of the experiences of being a black woman faculty member and the pitfalls and rewards of the tenure process which are particular to African-American women.

As well, there are a few ideal activities in which a mentor would participate. First, an ideal mentor would provide leadership and initiate the mentoring relationship. Second, a mentor would encourage and serve as a guide in the mentee's effort to balance teaching, research, and service activities geared toward tenure. Next, the mentor would advocate for the mentee within the department and around campus. Last, the mentor would provide information about the tenure process and critical feedback about the mentee's tenure focused activities.

As the literature suggests, mentoring was of prime importance to the participants in this study. When they existed, mentors assisted the participants through the tenure process by guiding activities, reading the "language" of the academy, and providing support. What varied from the literature was the importance of having a mentor who was a black woman. The literature suggests that race and gender matter little in mentoring. This appears to be true, but only if faced with the option of having no mentor at all. However, according to the participants, if given a choice, the overwhelming majority would choose an African-American woman. Those participants who had black women as mentors realized they had a resource who could provide information (albeit anecdotal) specific to their existence in the academy. They had a resource who not only understood but who most likely had experienced similar examples and patterns of racist and sexist behavior in academia. This was something that a white faculty member, male or female, could not offer. They could be empathetic if they acknowledged the existence of racism and sexism, but the deep-rooted understanding that comes from experience simply was not present. And although there is an argument that white women have experienced sexism, they have not experienced the type of sexism peculiar to black women, one that is rooted and laced with racism.

The Trilogy: Racism, Sexism, and the Politics of Singularity

There were countless examples of blatant racism and sexism faced by each of these women. Unlike the familiar "isolated incidences," some of the participants faced the "ism" on a day-to-day basis due to events that took place on campus. Four of the participants engaged in department and institution-wide battles with their colleagues about the treatment they received. These battles took place during the pre-tenure years, adding an interesting dimension to the dynamics of the tenure process.

Among the stories was a theme of a new type of racism which looked nothing like the "old" racism. While there were a couple of examples of name calling or other obvious forms of differential treatment (like Gayle's colleague moving along the tenure track more quickly than she, and Eloise's provost's unprecedented request for outside letters in the promotions phase), there were many more examples of very subtle, very covert acts of exclusion or challenges to the women's individual contributions and value to the department.

Inez best expressed the feelings, but each of the women were familiar with the differential treatment they received. There was a sense that there was a "new" form of racism which permeated the tenure process. The "old" form of racism was such that African-American women and other people of color would be subject to name calling, open and deliberate forms of differential treatment such as differences in pay, teaching assignments, or simply the refusal to hire black women and other minorities as faculty. It was overt activity in that the racist and sexist reasoning behind the activity was openly proclaimed and hostile. There was no need to hide the activity because racism was common practice and accepted in and around the United States.

The "new" form of racism has the same effect: fewer African-American women are hired as faculty, promoted, *and* tenured. There remains a difference in pay and faculty assignments. However, the rationale behind the activity is not openly racist or sexist because it is no longer common practice or acceptable to be openly racist or sexist in American society. But it is acceptable to be covertly racist and sexist. In other words, as long as the *stated* rationale has nothing to do with race or gender and the effect is disparate, as opposed to differential, the activity is seen as okay. The treatment is the same across race and gender but the impact of the treatment is different.

For example, it was clear to each of the participants that others in their respective departments had more information about the workings and rules of the tenure process. There were stories upon stories of the women finding out about opportunities or tenure requirements from their colleagues at the last minute. There were specific stories about white faculty members getting or having information about the tenure process before the participants.

Another example is the myth that simply doing one's work will earn a black woman faculty member tenure. The tenure process outlines a set of guidelines for teaching, research, and service which defines faculty work and faculty rewards. It makes sense that everyone has the same guidelines to follow and the process is predictable. But this is not the case. This idea ties into the notion that the tenure process is a game that has to be played by a set of unwritten rules which are known by or told only to a particular set of people based on race and gender. Since the game is not openly acknowledged, neither are unwritten rules. Thus cries about differential treatment within the game have little effect. When there is a lack of acknowledgement of a formal game, there are no formal rules to disseminate or follow.

Although the women, save two, were not hired to teach "minority issues," there was an expectation that they would work and mentor minority students. The expectations were internally and externally rooted. The women themselves thought they were expected to mentor and keep abreast of minority students. The department members made their expectations known by steering minority students in the direction of the African-American women faculty. Normally, this would not be problematic except that the time spent mentoring the students took time away from research and was not counted toward the participants' teaching and service activities. Mentoring was an inherent part of doing business as a black faculty member.

Tied to this was the idea that the women were the "minority representative" on most committees. There was an overwhelming feeling of being sought out more often for service opportunities, opportunities that would take time away from research endeavors. Only Rachel and Wilma put labels on the feelings: "institutional mammy" and "token," respectively.

Black women faculty are a unique group. They face the impact of race and gender in the tenure process. These women agreed that they are singled out to participate in more service activities, excluded from internal mentoring opportunities, and often targeted as hypersensitive or forces not to be reckoned with on campus. As a result, oftentimes the women were forced to discover and figure out the tenure game alone. Any complaints made by the participants were seen as noncollegial and the women were seen as individualist, traders, or, at minimum, non-team players.

The literature on African-American feminist thought best encompasses every aspect of the trilogy: racism, sexism, and the politics of singularity. African-American feminist thought ties together the trilogy as it is experienced by black women in the academy. Whether or not the participants welcomed it, each of the women (save Hope) was seen as having a particular role on campus. Whether it was the token, the mammy, the fighter, the young sex object, the servant, or the one who should just be grateful to be in the academy, it took some time for these women to be recognized as scholars and professionals.

Many of the negative experiences would not have happened had the participants not been black women. For example, had Jasmine been a white woman or a male, her colleague would have been less likely to question the office visits of the black male students. Had Linda or Rachel been white women or males, they likely would not have had scores of minority and female students jockeying for their time. Had any of the participants been white women, they might not have had to play the role of department housekeeper, their very existence being one who has to clean up the mess made by the department. As can be seen from the data, the black women served as the token in the department to show a commitment to diversity where there was none prior to their arrival on campus. They were used as pawns to recruit more faculty and students of color to often hostile environments. They also served as mentors to the previously non-mentored minority students and as the minority voice/department representative who took on unwanted service opportunities.

The Sista' Network

Six of the women felt a sense of isolation within their respective institutions. This isolation was due to the fact that they were the only, or one of a few, African-American women faculty on campus. The remaining three, though they did not personally feel it, recognized that others were isolated. Each felt that a strong mentoring or networking relationship on campus would have helped them to overcome that sense of isolation. In fact, what saved them was a small support network off campus. Each of the participants agreed that it was essential to have a support system both on and off campus. At minimum, African-American women should have someone, a family member or a girlfriend, with whom they can check in and connect. Having a network or support system was essential because it helped to cure isolation, provided the black woman faculty member with back-up in the event that dilemmas or controversies arose, helped the faculty member to learn the rules of the game, provided an opportunity to share work, and have one's work valued, and sometimes produced mentors. It appears from the data that each of the women had an off-campus network of black women with whom they commiserated, shared ideas, and published.

The networks are not hard to find, although they are not widely publicized. The networks developed underground, so to speak. Black women met as graduate students within the same institutions and continued supportive peer relationships after graduation. Some continued a mentoring relationship with black faculty from their undergraduate or graduate institutions. Others met at conferences and formed lasting collegial relationships. Still others met more informally through word of mouth.

Although there are discipline-based organizations for faculty of color, there are fewer organization for black women faculty across disciplines in general. The closest is an occasional conference such as Black Women in the Academy, sponsored by the African American Women's Institute at Howard University, held in 1995 and 1999. The conference brought together thousands of black women who learned, taught, and worked as administrators in academic institutions across the United States and abroad. It provided a forum for black women to get together, share ideas, and seek assistance, precisely what the Sista' Network should do. Sista' Networks can be formal or informal and should meet regularly and make efforts to pull other black women into the fold.

It is clear from the data that black women cannot leave their existence and survival in the academy up to the willingness of the establishment. Black women cannot rely on department chairs and other administrators to protect their interests and guide them along. Thus it is imperative to continue to mentor and network with other black women.

Other issues in the data became clear as well. Black women still "back bite" one another on their home campuses. They see each other in the hallways of the ivy tower and "forget from where they came." On campus they rarely speak to one another, offer assistance, work together, or take the time to commiserate. For some reason, it appears that it is easier for black women to connect off campus.

From one vantage point, they are too busy with other demands to make time for each other. From another, they view each other as the competition, because they *know* that there cannot be too many of "them" in the same department or institution, particularly with tenure. The politics of singularity are such that being the only one, or one of the few black women on campus, can be stressful.

Guiding Principles for African-American Women Faculty

If one looks at the data presented, black women were treated badly (or with indifference) regardless as to whether they helped other black women. If this is true, then it could be more advantageous and less stressful if black women chose to assist one another. There are several ways to ensure that this is done. From the data, 12 guiding principles emerged that can make the career of African-American women faculty more bearable, even successful. These principles can be used to form a game plan for new black women faculty members embarking upon the tenure process.

These guidelines are enumerated as individual tasks for faculty. The principles can be a directive of sorts and can be completed like a checklist. Deans and department chairs will find these guidelines useful as well. By taking the lead in offering these opportunities to faculty, deans and chairs can assist new faculty in effectively preparing for the tenure process.

1) Develop a Philosophical Framework

It is imperative that as a black woman you develop a philosophical framework that is rooted in passion. It is necessary to be passionate about the work you do. The passion enables you to continue the work through the rough times inherent in the tenure process. Developing a passion-based philosophical framework does more than drive your tenure activities. It can also serve as the foundation for a successful career. When your ideas and scholarship are challenged, simply refer back to your framework and refocus. If you are given work which is outside of your set agenda, you can say, "Thanks, but no thanks" and move on.

This needs to be done prior to entering a faculty position. Upon entering the academy as a faculty member, you need to have a clearly defined personal agenda. You need to be clear about who you are as an individual, as a professional, and as a scholar. You need to understand what *you* deem to be your role in the academy. Once this is done, you will be able to set a professional agenda and stick to it. As a result, you should be able to organize and negotiate all tenure-based activities to further your agenda.

2) Meet With the Department Chair and Dean

Within a month of being on campus (it is better even to do this before the semester begins), make an appointment with the department chair and school dean. The purpose of these meetings should be twofold. First, the meeting provides an opportunity for your chair and your dean to know your name and your face. Use this as an opportunity for them to learn about you and your research agenda. A few weeks before your appointment, send them a short document (of no more than two pages) with relevant information which is specific enough so that they get an idea about the type of research that interests you, but general enough not to lock you into any specific topic. Also, ask whether the chair or dean can put you in touch with any other faculty on (or off) campus who may be interested in the same research topics.

Second, the meetings should allow you to get as much detailed information on the tenure process as possible. Go into the meeting with specific questions.

- Does the department and/or school have a ranking order for publications?

- Does a book need to be published prior to tenure? If so, how many?
- Is there a committee assignment that fits within your research agenda?
- Are annual evaluations used toward mini-tenure and ultimately toward tenure?
- Are there specific steps and timelines for the tenure process?

Do not rely on new faculty orientations to provide information for this process. Instead, look at such activities as one piece of a myriad of useful information.

In addition to this meeting, meet less formally but frequently with your department chair, at minimum once per semester. Take these opportunities to inform your chair about the progress of your research agenda and to get feedback on your writing and teaching performance. One word of caution: If your department chair is inactive, do not go around him or her. Engage the chair in discussion, but find out who in the department holds the power. This can be done by watching to whom the chair listens, to whom the chair is responsive, and to whom other departmental colleagues look for leadership.

3) Set a Research Agenda

Set a research agenda before you arrive on campus and act on it immediately. Mentors in the field can assist you in developing a game plan. Find out from the department chair or school dean what type of publishing is appropriate for tenure (i.e., which type has greater value at your school) and create a timeline to begin sending out articles within six months of arriving on campus (make sure to have a mentor or senior colleague read the articles before submission). If at all possible, consider submitting at least two by the end of your first year on campus. Starting your research agenda early gives you a minimum of two articles in circulation when it is time for your first yearly evaluation. If you continue at this rate, you will have a sufficient amount of publications prior to mini-tenure to be viewed as "on the right track."

4) Ask for a Reduced Teaching Load

Ask your dean or chair to assign you a reduced teaching load during the first year of appointment. This should be negotiated when accepting the offer to join the faculty. When securing teaching assignments, you should develop and teach courses that fit your priorities and interests. However, you should also consider courses that broaden your teaching profile and encourage collegial connections such as multidisciplinary or team-taught courses. Seek support for teaching development through campus workshops, faculty grants for teaching, and the teaching and learning center.

5) Write Grants and Apply for Fellowships

Write grants and apply for fellowships before your third year mini-tenure. Grants and fellowships can provide you with release time and funds to conduct research. The academic affairs, grants and research, or faculty development offices on campus may be able to assist you in finding internal and external funds. The campus library may be able to help as well. Also consider making conference attendance part of your research or grant work and include conference costs and travel expenses into grants applications.

6) Decide if You Will Be the Minority Voice

Decide before you get on campus whether you are willing to be the minority voice in your department or institution. You will be pushed, persuaded, and cajoled when you arrive to mentor minority students and fill the void (read: minority slot) on committees. Whatever you decide, know that there will be repercussions either way, so choose service activities carefully. Protect your research agenda and stick to your decision.

7) Balance Teaching, Research, and Service

Regardless of institution type, teaching, research, and service are not equally weighted and must be balanced accordingly, with research given the bulk of your time. Although it might sound unrealistic, a suggested formula is to spend 55%–60% of your time on research and 25%–30% of your time on teaching. Service (both on and off campus) and networking should make up no more than 10%–20% of your schedule. Adhering to this agenda means you will spend a great deal of time working at your academic career; perhaps more than you originally anticipated.

Even faculty at teaching-oriented institutions can justify putting scholarship first. By starting your academic career with a heavy emphasis on research and publishing, you should get an early nod as to when you have reached the expected level of publishing for tenure. At this time you can shift the balance of your workload. When scholarship is your primary focus, you can develop and teach courses that further your research agenda. This makes it appear as if you are placing a heavier emphasis on teaching when in fact you are doing both teaching and research simultaneously. Also network and do service strategically by serving on a committee that is related to your research (also consider presenting your research at professional/disciplined-based conferences). Showcasing your research accomplishments will simultaneously get you recognition, outside support (read: outside letters for tenure), and highlight your department and home institution.

8) Be Good at What You Do

Make sure that you are up-to-date on new research and innovative teaching ideas. Update your courses. Send out only your best work, free of errors and professional in appearance. You must remember to be professional but approachable at all times.

9) Be Collegial

In addition to saying "Good morning" and Good afternoon," share your ideas with your colleagues and ask them about theirs. Ask them about any work they may have in progress. Engage them in discussions about current tends in the literature. Offer to be a guest speaker in a colleague's class (have a topic in mind that fits within the course parameters). Offer to give a brown-bag lunch talk on your research topic. Do what it takes to stay on track with your research agenda *and* to be seen as a team player.

10) Remember That the Tenure Process Is a Proactive Process

Document everything that happens that is job related, from the day you accept the job until the day you leave. Consider keeping a journal. Start your tenure file the first day in your new office (or sooner if the institution does not give you an office right away). Keep a record of all activity, both negative and positive. If it is negative, talk to someone and get help and support.

11) Learn to Politic and Do It Often

Tenure is a political process. If you are not politically inclined, take heed. This can be done by attending on-campus workshops, award ceremonies, and receptions, especially when your department or a colleague is sponsoring or being recognized at the event. Consider this the networking and collegial part of the tenure process. You do not have to, and should not, attend every event. Be selective and be seen.

In addition, remember that politicking must occur off campus as well. Attend regional and national conferences. If there is a discipline-based professional organization that does good work, volunteer to be on a committee. This will help you meet people in the field and garner support for your tenure bid (remember the outside letters). You can also use this opportunity to find a mentor.

12) Find a Mentor as Early in the Tenure Process as Possible

You must have someone senior to assist you in the tenure process. The ideal is to have a mentor in your discipline to show you how to advance in your field. You should also have an on-campus mentor to help you move through the institution-specific aspects of the tenure process. Lastly, do not forget to have a support network of African-American women to help guide you through the process of being a black woman faculty member.

Remember that all too often African-American women (and other women of color) do not have African-American female mentors in the academy. If there are other African-American women on campus, they are often faced with the same dilemmas and have to perform the same balancing act. This often leaves African-American women with women or men of other races and ethnicities as mentors. Although they may empathize, they have little direct understanding of the daily battles and struggles faced by African-American women.

There is some conversation within the academy that this is a generational issue. As more African-American women enter the academy as faculty, more mentors will be cultivated. At some point the numbers will match up and there will no longer be a lack of mentors. Only time will tell if these conversations are valid and additional research should be conducted in this area.

Conclusion: Six Years Later

This book originated as a study for my doctoral dissertation. I have kept in touch with almost all of the women who participated in this study. Much has changed for many of the participants since 2000 when this research was conducted. Gayle, Eloise, Hope, and Linda remain at their respective institutions and continue to publish. Jasmine remains at the same institution, and she earned tenure about a year after the study was completed. Wilma remains at her institution and took a well-deserved sabbatical. The others have made significant changes.

Shortly after the study was completed, Rachel started getting hints from her department that she would not be successful in her bid for tenure even though she completed mini-tenure successfully. She immediately put out feelers and left her institution. She went to a smaller, more prestigious institution that hired her as a tenured faculty member with an increase in rank. Rachel has reported that she is very happy at her new institution. She has published and continues to mentor students of color.

Inez left her institution for a more prestigious institution. She is currently on a faculty with several other African Americans. Inez continues to publish and mentor students. She reports that she is happy and feels valued at the institution.

Wendy took a sabbatic leave and subsequently left her institution and faculty life. She is currently a high-ranking administrator at another small institution in another part of the country. She reports that she is not happy as an administrator and may return to faculty life in the near future.

Shortly after meeting the participants, Thelma secured a non-tenure track faculty position at a small college in New England (she instead had a long-term contract). She subsequently became a department chair and remained as faculty for two and a half years. Thelma is currently an academic dean at a midsize state institution in New England. She reports that she is extremely happy in her position and has no plans to return to faculty life in the immediate future.

The tenure process is difficult and time-consuming for all involved, and it should not be made more lenient, or more difficult, for anyone. The process is the process, and it exists to provide job security, protect the rights of faculty members, and provide a mechanism or process for determining who should be privy to that security and protection. It has been said that the process is straightforward; those who do well or excel at the requirements set forth by the institution will earn tenure. This standard is fine when the process is clearly defined, structured, attainable, and fair. What can be seen from this data, however, is that while the process may work and be attainable, it is not clearly defined, well structured, or fair.

Institution-specific, written, detailed, self-explanatory information about the tenure process is difficult, if not impossible, to find. The information or rules that can be found are often very general in order to accommodate discipline-specific requirements. Such flexibility is important as there are differences in teaching pedagogies, research methodologies, and standards across disciplines. However, when the lack of specificity or ambiguity is used as a gatekeeper to tenure, one which has a disparate impact of a racist and sexist nature, then the process is inherently unfair.

If what Inez says is true, the game is one that cannot be played or won by following the written rules since there are none. If that is the case, then it is a racket, as Gayle pointed out, and not a game. Given a fair opportunity, structure, and support, almost anyone can survive and thrive during the tenure process and ultimately achieve tenure. Hence the argument for mentoring and institutional support for faculty development. A fair opportunity, however, means that everyone is given the same rules, the same level of support, and is judged based on the same criteria.

The goal is not for everyone to earn tenure. It is not a realistic outcome, nor is it desirable or economically practical for everyone to get tenure. Institutions spend upward of two million dollars per tenured faculty member on salaries over the course of their tenure careers. It makes sense that not everyone can or will be tenured because of the cost to institutions. As a result, institutions must find a way to contain those costs, and sometimes this is done by reducing the number of people who get tenure. This idea in and of itself is not problematic and can be achieved in different ways. One such way is for institutions to abolish tenure all together.[1] Although controversial, it will reduce the number of tenured faculty.

Institutions can make the process as clear and structured as possible and let equity rule. This means that institutions need to commit themselves to more specific and detailed criteria and make all such criteria known at the onset of employment. In addition, institutions must periodically monitor these requirements as technology and philosophies regarding scholarship expand.

Clearly, as the game changes and expands so must the rules. There are more women, more minorities, and more people of various religions and income levels in faculty positions than ever before. But be clear, while there are more, there are not nearly enough to mirror the changing society, particularly in the United States. An examination of the numbers tells us that the overwhelming majority of faculty, tenured and otherwise, are still white males. It is no longer acceptable to use the old boy network and its rules to determine who can play the game and enter the club. The good old boys are retiring and dying off. (The larger society, as well, is becoming less populated with the great descendants of George Washington and the passengers of the *Mayflower*.) If academia will not let tenure die, it should be changed at least; let it change and progress.

The information in this book has laid the foundation for that progression. It is hoped that by using the voices of African-American women who have participated in the process, the next generation of women who venture to negotiate the process will do so in an informed manner. It is imperative that one be prepared for all of the uncertainties found within the tenure process in order to make that negotiation successful.

Endnote

1) If institutions abolish tenure, they must find another way to protect and secure faculty appointments. Long-term contracts are one way to offer security to faculty.

Appendix A
Research Design and Methods

> Qualitative research in education, thus, maintains that the researcher's subjectivity is central. In consequence, the researcher's viewpoint and value judgments are deeply connected to the research . . . and what is being researched is impossible to separate. (Hara, 1995, p. 352)

The overall approach to this project is a phenomenological inquiry, a form of qualitative research. Since I sought to tell the stories of nine women, I wanted the narratives to be vividly rich and descriptive, like a well-written novel. This cannot be done through quantitative research methods and statistical analysis (Hara, 1995; Marshall & Rossman, 1999). Unlike quantitative methodology, which permits the researcher to look at cause and effect relationships, qualitative inquiry allowed me to focus on the interrelationship and interdependence of various factors (Mariano, 1995).

I interviewed nine women employed at seven different institutions. Each institution was a four-year, predominately and traditionally white college or university located on the east coast of the United States.

My methodology is nontraditional and feminist to the extent that while conducting the study, I interacted with the participants of my project and allowed them to define their realities in the academy. Historically, the researcher has been someone who was not a member of the participants' group. The researcher was known as the authority, observing the behaviors of the participants so that the behaviors could then be defined by the researcher (hooks, 1989). As a member of the participant group (the culture of black women) and not a member of the dominant group, I learned from and interacted with the women in the project as opposed to studying them (Rossman & Rallis, 1998). I saw the participants on an even, if not higher, plane than myself, as opposed to the traditional ideology of the researcher being superior to the participants. The two data collection methods I used for this study, correspondence and in-depth interviewing, enabled me to achieve my research goals (Letherby & Zdrodowski, 1995; Marshall & Rossman, 1999; Rossman & Rallis, 1998).

Letherby and Zdrodowski (1995) suggest that using correspondence as a research method allows the researcher and the participants to develop a rapport with one another. The authors report that correspondence as a methodology also allows for confidentiality in that people feel less exposed when they write to people initially rather than see them face-to-face. An early rapport can and did help during the interview process, which was the second stage of this project.

The correspondence methods used during the first stage of contact and data collection were email and letter writing. Letters were sent to 21 black women faculty asking for participation in the project. The women selected as participants fit within the sampling categories and were available within the project time schedule. Eleven women were initially selected. One participant withdrew in October 1998. In January 2000, the tape containing the data for another participant was inadvertently destroyed.

Next, a list of questions was sent to each of the participants requesting general demographic information about themselves and the institutions in which they work. I asked them to respond to three broad questions regarding their academic career, the tenure process, and their thoughts about how race, ethnicity, and gender were related to or dictated their experiences in those two areas. Emails and letters were used for clarification and follow up.

Writing letters and responding to email inquiries helped me to collect data and build a rapport with the interviewees. By the time I met these women in person, I felt like I knew them, and they me. Some of them greeted me with handshakes, and by the end we hugged to close the interview. As bell hooks (1989) stated, "Writing . . . enabled me to look at my past from a different perspective and to use this knowledge as a means of self-growth and change in a practical way" (p. 159). As the writer, I was empowered because I was allowed to look at the experiences of the participants critically and within the particular context of exploring the interrelationship among their race and ethnicity, gender, and the tenure process (Letherby & Zdrodowski, 1995).

In-depth interviewing was the second data collection method utilized. Since I expected to learn from and not study the participants, I used the *dialogic* style of interviewing because it allows for a sharing of ideas and information (Rossman & Rallis, 1998). Both the researcher and the participant develop an understanding of the subject matter together.

> Typically, qualitative in-depth interviews are much more like conversations than formal events with predetermined response categories. The researcher explores a few general topics to help uncover the participant's meaning perspective, but otherwise respects how the participant frames and structures the responses . . . the participant's perspective on the phenomenon of interest should unfold as the participant views it, not as the researcher views it. (Marshall & Rossman, 1999, p. 80)

Marshall and Rossman (1999) agree that in-depth interviewing helps meet this goal. Interviewing allowed the participants to provide their understandings of how the topics relate to their experiences and vice versa. There are three types of in-depth interviewing: the informal conversation-like interview, which is more like a conversation between two people about a particular topic; the general interview, which has a great deal of structure regarding the order of the questions and the type of response solicited; and the open-ended interview, which allows for questions to be asked in any order with allowances for follow-up questions not originally in the question scheme to clarify points of confusion (Mariano, 1995; Peirce, 1995). My interviews were a combination of each of these typologies. To do a thorough job, my interviews had to be flexible enough to follow up on important points that arose during the conversations. I kept my interview questions relatively flexible, and the discussions took off in many different but relevant directions.

I conducted one two- to four-hour interview with each of the participants. The interviews took place between October and December 1998. The questions asked about very specific experiences during the tenure process. I asked the participants to tell stories about their experiences and to elaborate on the meaning of those experiences. Seven interviews were conducted in the participants' faculty offices on their home campuses. Two participants requested that we meet off campus. Jasmine and I met in a restaurant near campus. I interviewed Gayle in her home.

Both correspondence and in-depth interviewing have weaknesses as data collection methods. For the purposes of my study, however, the weaknesses did not outweigh the strengths outlined above. The major weakness for both methods is that they produce volumes of information, some of which may prove to be irrelevant. Another weakness is that the credibility of what a person is saying about herself in a letter or an interview may be questioned. Although it is possible that a participant may lie or tend to over- or misrepresent herself in an interview, this is no more likely to happen in an interview than on a survey (Harrison & Lyon, 1993; Letherby & Zdrodowski, 1995; Marshall & Rossman, 1999; Mykhalovskiy, 1996). And while there was great deal of information produced, all of it was useful in some respect, either as background or clarifying information.

Regardless of the method of data collection used, it is imperative that the information collected be credible and plausibly representative of the greater population of participants. Therefore, it is necessary to have a methodology for selecting the participants. This methodology is commonly referred to as sampling.

Snowball and opportunistic sampling were the two approaches used in this study to select participants.

Snowball, or chain sampling, takes place when participants are found by word of mouth (Patton, 1990). For example, once one participant is secured, that participant informs the researcher that he or she knows of another individual who meets the researcher's needs or criteria. Snowballing also occurs when the researcher asks, "This is my topic, who should I talk to?" Depending upon the topic, "The chain of recommended informants will typically diverge initially as many possible sources are recommended, then converge as a few key names get mentioned over and over" (Patton, 1990, p. 176).

Opportunistic sampling happens when the researcher takes advantage of a "chance" meeting with a person who would make a good participant (Patton, 1990). This type of sampling can also occur when the researcher finds himself or herself in a position to do on-the-spot observation that is applicable to the study. In other words, the sampling is not planned; it is merely an opportunity which presents itself. "Opportunistic sampling takes advantage of whatever unfolds as it unfolds" (Patton, 1990, p. 179).

Both sampling methods worked well for my project. In fact, both snowball and opportunistic sampling had occurred in the preliminary stages of this research. Upon discussing my literature review with one participant, she remarked, "I know this author, we went to graduate school together. She'd be great to interview. She is now at [a small New England] college." Two weeks later, someone else showed me a newspaper advertisement for a woman who was speaking locally about race and the tenure process. I went to the seminar and the speaker agreed to talk to me about being a participant in my project. During an interview, one participant took me around her department looking for other black women for me to interview. These are excellent examples of opportunistic and sampling methodology in action.

References

Hara, K. (1995). Quantitative and qualitative research approaches in education. *Education, 115*(3), 351–356.

Harrison, B., & Lyon, E. S. (1993). A note on ethical issues in the use of autobiography in sociological research. *Sociology, 27*(1), 101–109.

hooks, b. (1989). *Talking back: Thinking feminist, thinking black.* Cambridge, MA: South End Press.

Letherby, G., & Zdrodowski, D. (1995). "Dear researcher": The use of correspondence as a method within feminist qualitative research. *Gender and Society, 9*(5), 576–593.

Mariano, C. (1995). The qualitative research process. In L. A. Talbot, *Principles and practice of nursing research* (pp. 463–491). St. Louis, MO: Mosby.

Marshall, C., & Rossman, G. B. (1999). *Designing qualitative research* (3rd ed.). Thousand Oaks, CA: Sage.

Mykhalovskiy, E. (1996). Reconsidering table talk: Critical thoughts on the relationship between sociology, autobiography, and self-indulgence. *Qualitative Sociology, 19*(1), 131–151.

Patton, M. Q. (1990). *Qualitative evaluation and research methods* (2nd ed.). Thousand Oaks, CA: Sage.

Peirce, A. G. (1995). Measurement instruments. In L. A. Talbot, *Principles and practice of nursing research* (pp. 292–316). St. Louis, MO: Mosby.

Rossman, G. B., & Rallis, S. F. (1998). *Learning in the field: An introduction to qualitative research.* Thousand Oaks, CA: Sage.

Appendix B
Sample Interview Questions

The Tenure Process

- **Teaching, Research, Service**

    Were decisions to teach a particular class, research a topic, or participate in service activities made based on whether the activities would help with tenure?

    Did you speak to anyone about teaching, research, and service priorities? If so, who? When?

- **Mentoring/Networking**

    Was the tenure process explained to you? When? By whom? How? What were you told?

    What or who helped you through the tenure process? Describe what the person did to help.

    Did you have support for your teaching, research, and service efforts? From your colleagues? Staff in the department? Your chair? Your dean?

    Do you belong to any institutional, regional, or national organizations (related to academe)? What are they? Are you active?

    Do you attend conferences or networking functions? If yes, which ones?

- **The Day-to-Day Experiences**

    Describe a high/low of your experience in the tenure process thus far (i.e., tell me a tenure story).

    Which aspects of being a faculty member give you the most gratification (teaching, research, service)? Why?

    Are you the only black woman faculty member in your department or institution? The only faculty of color at the institution?

Do you perceive there to be barriers to tenure? For whom? Placed by whom? What kind?

Have you encountered any barriers thus far during the tenure process? Placed by whom? What kind?

Has the tenure process been a struggle for you? In what way?

Do you perceive there to be tension or hardship in the tenure process? For whom? What are those hardships?

What aspects of the tenure process have created the most tension or hardship for you? Why?

What aspects of the tenure process have been the most rewarding? Why?

The Role Race, Gender, and Class Play in the Participant's Bid for Tenure

How do you see (what meaning do you make of) the relationship among your race, class, and gender and your efforts to get tenure?

Sista' Network

Do you have a network of black women faculty to talk to about your/their experiences in the academy? If so, are they teaching at your institution or another? How did you meet?

Does it matter to you whether your mentor is a black woman faculty member? Why or why not? Do you have a preference?

Suggestions

If you had to repeat the tenure process (start all over again), would you do it again? Would you do anything differently? What and why? What wouldn't you change? Why?

Do you have any advice for new black women faculty?

Bibliography

Aguirre, A., Jr. (1995). The status of minority faculty in academe. *Equity and Excellence in Education, 28,* 63–68.

Aguirre, A., Jr., Martinez, R., & Hernandez, A. (1993). Majority and minority faculty perceptions in academe. *Research in Higher Education, 34*(3), 371–385.

Aisenberg, N., & Harrington, M. (1988). *Women of academe: Outsiders in the sacred grove.* Amherst, MA: University of Massachusetts Press.

Alexander, M. W. (1995). Black women in academia. In B. Guy-Sheftall (Ed.), *Words of fire: An anthology of African-American feminist thought* (pp. 454–460). New York, NY: The New Press. (Original work published 1972)

Alexander-Snow, M., & Johnson, B. J. (1999). Perspectives from faculty of color. In R. J. Menges & Associates, *Faculty in new jobs: A guide to settling in, becoming established, and building institutional support* (pp. 88–117). San Francisco, CA: Jossey-Bass.

Banks, A. (1998). Some people would say I tell lies. In A. Banks & S. P. Banks (Eds.), *Fiction and social research: By ice or fire* (pp. 167–178). Walnut Creek, CA: AltaMira Press.

Banks, S. P., & Banks, A. (1998). The struggle over facts and fictions. In A. Banks & S. P. Banks (Eds.), *Fiction and social research: By ice or fire* (pp. 11–32). Walnut Creek, CA: AltaMira Press.

Benjamin, L. (1997). Black women in the academy: An overview. In L. Benjamin (Ed.), *Black women in the academy: Promises and perils* (pp. 1–7). Gainesville, FL: University Press of Florida.

Blackwell, J. E. (1996). Faculty issues: The impact on minorities. In C. S. V. Turner, M. Garcia, A. Nora, & L. I. Rendon (Eds.), *Racial and ethnic diversity in higher education* (pp. 315–326). Needham Heights, MA: Simon and Schuster.

Braskamp, L. A., & Ory, J. C. (1994). *Assessing faculty work: Enhancing individual and institutional performance.* San Francisco, CA: Jossey-Bass.

Burgess, N. J. (1997). Tenure and promotion among African American women in the academy: Issues and strategies. In L. Benjamin (Ed.), *Black women in the academy: Promises and perils* (pp. 227–234). Gainesville, FL: University Press of Florida.

Byse, C., & Joughin, L. (1959). *Tenure in American higher education: Plans, practices, and the law.* Ithaca, NY: Cornell University Press.

Carter, D. J., & O'Brien, E. M. (1993). *Employment and hiring patterns for faculty of color* (Research Briefs, 4[6]). Washington, DC: American Council on Education, Division of Policy Analysis and Research.

Cole, J. B. (1993). *Conversations: Straight talk with America's sister president.* New York, NY: Doubleday.

Cole, J. B. (1995). Epilogue. In B. Guy-Sheftall (Ed.), *Word of fire: An anthology of African-American feminist thought* (pp. 549–552). New York, NY: The New Press.

Cole, J. B. (1997). *Ten years at Spelman: Reflections on a special journey.* Keynote address presented at the Otelia Cromwell Day Symposium at Smith College, Northampton, MA.

Collins, P. H. (1986). Learning from the outsider within: The sociological significance of black feminist thought. *Social Problems, 33*(6), S14–S32.

Collins, P. H. (2000). *Black feminist thought: Knowledge, consciousness, and the politics of empowerment* (2nd ed.). New York, NY: Routledge.

Cooper, A. J. (1995). The status of woman in America. In B. Guy-Sheftall (Ed.), *Words of fire: An anthology of African-American feminist thought* (pp. 44–50). New York, NY: The New Press. (Original work published 1892)

Fields, C. D. (1996). A morale dilemma. *Black Issues in Higher Education, 13*(17), 22–29.

Finkin, M. W. (1996). *The case for tenure.* Ithaca, NY: Cornell University Press.

Franklin, J. H. (1974). *From slavery to freedom: A history of Negro Americans* (4th ed.). New York, NY: Alfred A. Knopf.

Goodwin, C. D. (1995). Some tips on getting tenure. In A. L. DeNeef & C. D. Goodwin (Eds.), *The academic's handbook* (2nd ed., pp. 150–157). Durham, NC: Duke University Press.

Granger, M. W. (1993). A review of the literature on the status of women and minorities in the professoriate in higher education. *Journal of School Leadership, 3*(2), 121–135.

Graves, S. B. (1990). A case of double jeopardy? Black women in higher education. *Initiatives, 53,* 3–8.

Gregory, S. T. (1995). *Black women in the academy: The secrets to success and achievement.* New York, NY: University Press of America.

Grisham, J. (1996). *The runaway jury.* New York, NY: Doubleday.

Hawkins, H. (1979). University identity: The teaching research functions. In A. Oleson & J. Voss (Eds.), *The organization of knowledge in modern America, 1860–1920* (pp. 285–312). Baltimore, MD: Johns Hopkins University Press.

hooks, b. (1989). *Talking back: Thinking feminist, thinking black*. Cambridge, MA: South End Press.

Johnsrud, L. K. (1993). Women and minority faculty experiences: Defining and responding to diverse realities. In J. Gainen & R. Boice (Eds.), *New directions for teaching and learning: No. 53. Building a diverse faculty* (pp. 3–16). San Francisco, CA: Jossey Bass.

Johnsrud, L. K., & Des Jarlais, C. D. (1994). Barriers to tenure for women and minorities. *Review of Higher Education, 17*(4), 335–353.

Joseph, G. (1995). Black feminist pedagogy and schooling in capitalist white America. In B. Guy-Sheftall (Ed.), *Words of fire: An anthology of African-American feminist thought* (pp. 462–471). New York, NY: The New Press. (Original work published 1988)

Kilbourn, B. (1999). Fictional theses. *Educational Researcher, 28*(9), 27–32.

Krizek, R. L. (1998). Lessons: What the hell are we teaching the next generation anyway? In A. Banks & S. P. Banks (Eds.), *Fiction and social research: By ice or fire* (pp. 89–113). Walnut Creek, CA: AltaMira Press.

Leaming, D. R. (1998). *Academic leadership: A practical guide to chairing the department*. Bolton, MA: Anker.

Leap, T. L. (1995, March 31). Tenure, discrimination, and African American faculty. *Journal of Blacks in Higher Education, 7*, 103–105.

Locke, M. E. (1997). Striking the delicate balances: The future of African American women in the academy. In L. Benjamin (Ed.), *Black women in the academy: Promises and perils* (pp. 340–346). Gainesville, FL: University Press of Florida.

Lorde, A. (1984). *Sister outsider*. Berkeley, CA: The Crossing Press.

Malveaux, J. (1998). Retaining master jugglers. *Black Issues in Higher Education, 15*(1), 40.

Mariano, C. (1995). The qualitative research process. In L. A. Talbot, *Principles and practice of nursing research* (pp. 463–491). St. Louis, MO: Mosby.

Mazon, M. R., & Ross, H. (1990). Minorities in the higher education pipeline: A critical view. *Western Journal of Black Studies, 14*(3), 159–165.

McKay, N. Y. (1997). A troubled peace: Black women in the halls of the white academy. In L. Benjamin (Ed.), *Black women in the academy: Promises and perils* (pp. 11–22). Gainesville, FL: University Press of Florida.

Metzger, W. P., O'Toole, J., & Glazer, P. M. (1979). *Tenure*. Washington, DC: American Association for Higher Education.

Mitchell, J. (1983). Visible, vulnerable, and viable: Emerging perspectives of a minority professor. In J. H. Cones, III, J. F. Noonan, & D. Janha (Eds.), *New directions for teaching and learning: No. 16. Teaching minority students* (pp. 17–28). San Francisco, CA: Jossey-Bass.

Moses, Y. (1989). *Black women in academe: Issues and strategies* (Project on the status and education of women). Washington, DC: Association of American Colleges.

Moses, Y. (1997). Black women in academe: Issues and strategies. In L. Benjamin (Ed.), *Black women in the academy: Promises and perils* (pp. 23–37). Gainesville, FL: University Press of Florida.

Olsen, D., Maple, S. A., & Stage, F. K. (1995). Women and minority faculty job satisfaction: Professional role interests, professional satisfactions, and institutional fit. *Journal of Higher Education, 66*(3), 267–293.

O'Toole, J., Van Alstyne, W. W., & Chait, R. (1979). *Three views: Tenure*. New York, NY: Change Magazine Press.

Park, S. M. (1996). Research, teaching, and service: Why shouldn't women's work count? *Journal of Higher Education, 67*(1), 46–84.

Peterson, S. (1990). Challenges for black women faculty. *Initiatives, 53*(1), 33–36.

Ruffins, P. (1997). The fall of the house of tenure. *Black Issues in Higher Education, 14*, 19–26.

Sorcinelli, M. D. (2000). Principles of good practice: Supporting early-career faculty: Guidance for deans, department chairs, and other academic leaders. In R. E. Rice, M. D. Sorcinelli, & A. E. Austin (Eds.), *Heeding new voices: Academic careers for a new generation* (New Pathways Working Paper Series No. 7). Washington, DC: American Association for Higher Education.

Smith, B. (1995). Some home truths on the contemporary black feminist movement. In B. Guy-Sheftall (Ed.), *Words of fire: An anthology of African-American feminist thought* (pp. 254–267). New York, NY: The New Press. (Original work published 1983)

Tierney, W. G., & Rhodes, R. A. (1993). *Faculty socialization as cultural process: A mirror of institutional commitment* (ASHE-ERIC Higher Education Report No. 93[6]). Washington, DC: The George Washington University, School of Education and Human Development.

Turner, C. S. V., & Myers, S. L., Jr. (2000). *Faculty of color in academe: Bittersweet success.* Needham Heights, MA: Allyn & Bacon.

U.S. Department of Education, National Center for Education Statistics. (1994). *Faculty and instructional staff: Who are they and what do they do?* (NCES 94-346). Survey Report of the 1993 National Study of Postsecondary Faculty. Washington, DC: Author.

Whicker, M. L., Kronenfeld, J. J., & Strickland, R. A. (1993). *Getting tenure* (Vol. 8). Thousand Oaks, CA: Sage.

Index

Affirmative action, 3, 15, 22, 25, 26
African-American (black) feminist thought, 3, 4, 6, 29–32, 39, 117
African-American (black) students, 22, 29, 32, 55, 69
African-American (black) women faculty, 1, 3–6, 17, 18, 21, 23, 24, 26, 27, 29, 31, 32, 37–39, 90, 96, 106, 107, 109, 111, 117, 118–120, 132, 138
Aguirre, A., Jr., 15, 22, 23, 25, 27
Aisenberg, N., 12, 13

Benjamin, L., 2, 3, 10, 11, 13, 17, 32
Black Women in the Academy conference, 119
Burgess, N. J., 10, 11, 24, 25

Carter, D. J., 17, 18, 19, 32
Class, 2, 30, 31, 39, 42, 43, 80–81, 84, 138
Cole, J. B., 3, 4, 5, 23, 24
College and university presidents, 8, 23, 52, 53, 80, 91
Collegiality, 13, 25, 43, 54, 60, 62–64, 77, 107, 109, 111–113
Collins, P. H., 29, 30, 31, 32

Deans, 82, 107, 120

Department chairs, 9, 29, 107, 112, 119, 120
Des Jarlais, C. D., 3, 16, 28

Eloise, 41, 43, 47, 67, 74, 83–84, 92–94, 99–100, 109, 115, 127

Faculty development, 123
Faculty of color, 15, 16, 17, 18, 19, 20, 21, 22, 32, 66, 68, 71, 119, 137
Fields, C. D., 2, 3, 15, 16, 17, 22, 23, 24, 25, 26, 27, 28
Full-time faculty, 18

Gayle, 41, 43, 47–49, 52–53, 58–60, 63–64, 80, 94, 101–102, 103, 104–105, 113, 116, 127, 128, 134
Gender, 1, 2, 10, 12, 15, 16, 17, 24, 25, 26, 28, 30, 31, 39, 42, 43, 54, 75, 77, 80–81, 84, 85, 88, 110, 113, 114, 116, 117, 132, 133
Graves, S. B., 2, 3, 4, 24, 25, 26, 29
Gregory, S. T., 3, 17, 23, 29, 32
Guiding principles, 106, 120–126

Harrington, M., 12, 13
hooks, b., 30, 31, 32, 131, 132–133
Hope, 40, 43, 45, 46, 51–52, 53–54, 65, 67, 71–72, 74, 75, 79, 85, 89, 90, 96, 98, 117, 127

Imperfect narrative, 34–37
Inez, 40, 43, 44–45, 50–51, 52, 54, 60, 66, 67, 70, 72, 73–74, 78, 82–83, 85–87, 88–89, 91–92, 94–95, 100–101, 102, 110, 115, 127, 128
Isolation, 2, 3, 23–25, 35, 77–89, 93, 118

Jasmine, 40, 43, 45–46, 49–50, 51, 53, 54–58, 64–65, 68, 71, 76, 77–79, 84–85, 94, 95–97, 107, 118, 127, 134
Johnsrud, L. K., 3, 16, 27, 28

Kilbourn, B., 34, 36, 38
Kronenfeld, J. J., 9, 10, 13, 14

Linda, 40–41, 43, 44, 46, 65, 68–69, 74, 89, 95, 102, 118, 127
Locke, M. E., 6, 16, 22, 23, 25, 26, 27, 28, 29

Malveaux, J., 3
McKay, N. Y., 2, 16, 22, 23, 25, 29
Mentor, 22, 23, 26, 27, 29, 44, 61, 62, 69, 70–77, 78, 89, 91, 93, 94, 100, 102, 106, 107, 111, 113–115, 116, 117, 118, 119, 122, 123, 125, 126, 127, 138
Mentoring, 1, 3, 10, 12, 23, 26, 32, 43, 60, 62, 66, 69–77, 82, 88, 93, 111, 114, 117, 118, 119, 128, 137
Minority faculty, 2, 3, 15, 16, 29, 81
Minority students, 16, 22, 29, 55, 62, 116, 117, 118, 123

Moses, Y., 3, 6, 15, 16, 22, 23, 24, 25, 26, 27, 28
Myers, S. L., Jr., 25, 26

Networking, 4, 25–27, 89–94, 118, 124, 125, 137
New faculty, 7, 25, 34, 43, 80, 83, 96–102, 106, 109, 120, 122

O'Brien, E. M., 17, 18, 19, 32

Politics, 12, 13, 59, 77, 89
 of singularity, 115–118, 120
Provost, 8, 57, 83, 115
Publishing, 11, 22, 28, 42, 46, 70, 95, 122, 124

Qualitative research, 4, 37, 39, 99, 131, 133

Race, 1, 2, 15, 25, 28, 30, 31, 39, 41, 42, 43, 54, 68, 75, 77, 80–86, 87, 88, 92, 110, 116, 117, 126, 132, 133, 135, 138
Rachel, 41, 43, 45, 51, 60–63, 65–66, 68, 69–70, 72–73, 74–75, 76–77, 80–82, 87–88, 90, 92, 95, 96, 101, 103–104, 108, 117, 118, 127
Research, 1–3, 6–13, 16, 22, 26, 27–29, 32, 36, 37, 39, 46, 47, 51, 52, 58, 63–66, 70, 73, 74, 75, 81, 87, 88, 90, 91, 92, 93, 95–99, 101, 104, 106, 107, 108, 109–111, 112, 113, 114, 116, 117, 121, 122–123, 128, 132, 135
 institutions, 39, 40, 41, 43, 54, 65, 66, 96

Rhodes, R. A., 15, 16

Service, 2, 7, 9, 10, 11, 12, 13, 25, 27, 28, 29, 40, 42, 46, 47, 48, 49, 51, 52, 53, 64–69, 74, 80, 95–96, 98, 101, 103, 104, 106, 107, 108, 109–111, 113, 114, 116, 117, 118, 123, 124, 137
Sista' Network, 4, 5, 118–120, 138
Sorcinelli, M. D., 26
Strickland, R. A., 9, 10, 13, 14

Teaching, 3, 7, 9–13, 27, 28, 29, 40, 46, 47, 49, 51, 57, 58, 61, 64–69, 74, 80, 95, 96, 98, 101, 103, 104, 106, 107, 108, 109–111, 113, 114, 116, 117, 123, 124, 137
    evaluations, 7, 8, 46, 47, 65, 66, 72, 122
    institutions, 39, 64
Tenure, 3–9, 10, 12–14, 16, 17, 19, 22, 23, 27, 28, 32, 39, 40–52, 54, 56, 58, 60, 65, 68–71, 74, 75, 79, 82–84, 87–90, 93, 95–97, 99, 100, 103–109, 111–116, 120–125, 127–130, 137, 138
    game, 12, 32, 40, 107–109, 117
    mini-tenure, 7, 41, 45, 46, 63, 104, 108, 122, 123, 127
    pre-tenure, 15, 110, 115

process, 1, 4, 6, 7–10, 15, 17, 26, 27–29, 38, 40, 43–54, 59, 60, 62, 65, 71, 75, 80–81, 83, 92, 94, 97, 99, 101, 103, 106, 107, 108, 109, 111–113, 114, 115, 116, 117, 120, 121, 122, 125, 126, 128, 130, 132, 133, 134, 135, 137, 138
and promotion, 1, 7, 28, 40, 41, 45, 46, 47, 49, 50, 51, 52, 53, 58, 59, 63, 83, 84, 89, 90, 105, 108, 112, 113, 115
and unwritten rules, 4, 5, 9, 13, 53–54, 109, 116
Thelma, 39–40, 42–43, 44, 47, 48, 49, 51, 52, 53, 54, 59, 62, 64, 66, 69, 70, 73, 75, 77, 78, 79, 80, 81, 86, 87, 88, 89, 90, 92, 93, 94, 96, 102, 103, 105, 128
Tierney, W. G., 15, 16
Turner, C. S. V., 25, 26

Wendy, 41, 43, 44, 47, 50, 66–67, 71, 76, 84, 89, 97–98, 127
Whicker, M. L., 9, 10, 13, 14
White women faculty, 2, 17, 19, 89, 115, 118
Wilma, 40, 43, 47, 65, 67, 70, 72, 75, 77, 84, 89, 90–91, 98, 103, 109, 117, 127

Property of
Project INSPIRE